IS GOD ENDANGERED BY BELIEVERS?

A Critical Study of the Gap Between Religion and Real Faith

by Jean-François Six

Dimension Books
Denville, New Jersey 07834

Published by Dimension Books
P.O. Box 811, Denville, New Jersey 07834

This is a translation of *L'incroyance et la foi ne sont pas ce qu'on croit* by Jean-François Six (Paris: Editions du Centurion, 1979). This English translation was made by Salvator Attanasio.

Table of Contents

PREFACE

A sticker that is often seen on the rear bumpers of automobiles in the United States reads: "God Is Alive and Well." In France we cite statistics: God's rating is "rising" or "falling" and on occasion it plummets "to the lowest point." One of the primary concerns of opinion makers in Catholic circles (editors of Catholic media and spiritual directors) is to show, through figures, a good index of growth or of expansion or of renewal of the one whom we call God.

This book does not propose to prove the existence of God on the basis of reported successes and figures. Nor does it try to present an effective or mathematical demonstration for God's existence: it is not a standard manual of apologetics. But in no way does it disavow theology: not for a moment does the author forget that he has been a professor of theology for a very long time, and that, from the outset, he has never ceased searching for a rational justification of the act of faith.

Well, then, what kind of a book is it? Let us forewarn the reader: it is, as it were, a situated book, that is, it belongs in a current of thought. At the end of the last century Rome almost succeeded in imposing on the ensemble of Catholic clerics and people a sole form of theology, almost a sole expression of faith. By so doing it turned its back on the beginnings of the Church in which the Gospels were four and the Apostles twelve, and on the whole history of the Church in which there were various schools of theology. The bursting of the barriers of space and time, the major event of our epoch, and the subsequent occurrence of the many changes that we are observing are two events that have collided head-on with this monist centralization, and we are starting afresh to breathe, to savor different airs (I am speaking of music and of harmony), to love the notion that the Holy Spirit is not obligated to conform to a single mold. I know that I am immersed in a definite current of thought, a current that goes from Francis of Assisi to John XXIII by way of Charles de Foucauld and Thérèse of Lisieux, without forgetting Fénelon and de Caussade or Abbé Huvelin, the priest who had the deepest influence on me, the one thanks to whom I discovered, through his papers, Frances de Sales and Charles de Foucauld, but also Littré, the unbeliever. It was Abbé Huvelin who made me approach the shores where one pauses to listen and is open to dialogue.

In this current one learns first of all to keep watch, to cock an ear, to scan the night, to await the dawn. There are other currents, and I can, even without wishing to live within them, understand them and love them: the current, more headstrong, of youth and of morning; the current, triumphal and luminous, of noon and of summers; or still the current of eventide, that of remembrance and traditions. But on the map of faith and in the work of the Church, the fact is that I work at night, I am of the night. Dare I name some companions of the vigil such as I, at least, see them? In France, many of my brothers of the Mission de France, a goodly number of those of the Society of Jesus, from Michel de Certeau to François Varillon, by way of Pierre-Jean Labarrière and Bruno Ribes without, of course, forgetting the Dominicans M. D. Chenu and Jean-Pierre Jossua, or Maurice Bellet and Jean Sullivan, Madeleine Delbrel or France Quéré. The list is not restrictive and I am thinking, most particularly at this moment, and at one and the same time, not only of these known names but of all friends, unknown by name, yet so close and present.

He who says "night" does not say obscurity, still less darkness. In my office hangs a reproduction of a painting by Alfred Mannessier, a friend. This painting, entitled *Night,* dates from 1956, the year of my ordination. It is studded with spots of light. Yes, night is replete with signs; it is not an unfurling of unutterable shadows and of instinctive drives; it is the will to scan, to scrutinize. The watchers by night are very lucid seers, not sleep-walkers.

To participate in this current of thought is to have first and foremost this sense of realism proper to watchers by night: they must before all else learn that the moon is not made of green cheese. It is also in the darkness that one gets used to calling a spade a spade. At times the watchers by night appear—or they are thus caricatured—as pessimistic beings who are down in the dumps, or as polemicists who squabble in the shadows. It's nothing of the sort. To say in black and white that unbelief and faith are not what we believe or what we want to believe, is tantamount to taking stock, as it were, to warding off the danger of straying off course, to fixing anew the guiding stars. It does not signal a rejection of certitudes and beacons, it means simply to ask—tactfully—that one refrain from leaping recklessly into traps and lures.

To participate today in this current is also to understand that old-fashioned atheism with its own certitudes, is a creed outworn; and that agnosticism—the pride of a human being who, quite rightly, does not want to deceive himself or allow himself to be deceived—is a path that henceforth is the choice of many hearts and minds. It is to understand that the militancy which limits itself to spouting proclamations without specifying approaches weighs itself down and simply can't get off the ground. And this likewise applies to ideologies. It is to understand that paganism and pantheism are extremely intrusive thistles in the Christian field—hence those who applaud religious renewals would do well to reflect on this matter so as not to confuse the seers and the gurus with the Messiah. And they would also do well to read Louis Pauwels, who recently published a manifesto in which he asserts: "The future lies in the reactivation of a great paganism."

The watchers by night are the companions of the night. They are not at ease with instant "problem-solvers," with the "cocksure," with those who want to pierce the night by means of garish and artificial projectors, whether these projectors be "integralists," council activists, or revolutionaries. The watchers by night say: night exists, we have encountered it, and they do not want it to be short-circuited, to be cleared: night is not to be effaced. They even think that night emits an indispensable light and proffers a hope.

In the night, human beings lose their hardness; in the night it is no longer a question of measuring oneself against the sun and of wanting to jump over one's shadow. It is then that we dare to let the garments of our prejudices fall or to say that we have been mistaken; it is then that we dare to contradict ourselves. This book is an invitation to an experimental faith, humble and vulnerable, an invitation to a God who springs up in the life of a human being and in the history of humanity and who does it gently in the form of a murmur and of a sound, a God who does not furnish an explication but who becomes, lovingly and enthusiastically, caring of men, and gives them his Son—I was about to say his flesh and blood.

Faith is an invitation; faith is first and foremost of the order of love; it is to put trust in the One who one day put trust in you—and He is always the first to love. And faith is also the question: Why does He love? Why does He love humanity? Why does He love human beings and me among them? Why is He what He is?

Confronted, in the name of the Church, with this Word that comes from elsewhere, that transfixes and traverses me, I try to live this trust and this question together, to live with them. On a dark night. From day to day.

Jean-François Six

I

VALERIE
OR
A NEW WORLD

PORTRAIT OF VALERIE

Do you know Valerie? She's eighteen years old, willowy, always—or almost always—in jeans. She's "of today," marked by the new mentality which worms itself into her mind and her behavior. And this insinuation is effected through a thousand fine, invisible percussions that reach her like lasar beams, through the remarks of girlfriends and boyfriends, through what she hears from her transistor, most often tuned on, through the newspapers for young people that she leafs through. She receives all this informational output with an astonishing swiftness and she sorts it out in her own way. Valerie is a young feline unceasingly on the alert, unceasingly on the move. Her grandmother, delighted with her grand-daughter's development, observes her out of the corner of one eye and finds her freedom and vivaciousness vastly amusing.

Valerie has decided to work in July in order to earn the money necessary for travelling in August. She plans to go to Turkey with two girlfriends and a boyfriend. Why Istanbul and Cappodocia? "It's not the monuments that interest me nor the gimmicks *à la* Pierre Loti. Turkey is somewhat mysterious. India is too far for my purse. Afghanistan scares me somewhat. The Balearic Islands are for grandparents. Parents go to Spain. To each his culture." Valerie's father is a minor technician: "3,000 francs a month," says Valerie. He's a militant in his party and in his union. "He says that Marxism is a scientific theory and therefore true. Me, I'm not for theory; that locks you in." "What" is Valerie for? "For nothing," but then what? "Not for a 'cause,' not for a big gimmick, an ideology. I'm for 'playing it by ear.' Otherwise one lets oneself be had. Every time something goes wrong, somebody somehow manages to explain it to you. True, there are dissidents in the USSR, but it's because . . . ideology is always right, it always finds reasons so one is always obliged to accept the unacceptable. I often squabble with my dad over this. He's always wanting me to exercise patience, to wait, because everything will turn out all right in the end. Me, I'm for the here and now, the heres and nows in which one laughs at the same time and one bawls, not for the singing tomorrows. I tell my dad that tomorrows are a form of blackmail."

So Valerie is for today. To build tomorrow according to grand perspectives is not to her taste. She's afraid of those who set forth marvelous projects for the transformation of the world, projects similar to the beautiful, rationally planned cities in which the planners build impeccable avenues through the wilderness of forests. She's reticent about Brasilia and the trans-Amazonian route. The desire to choke the future in an iron collar of organizations strikes her as a worthless aspiration. She mistrusts architects who want to establish the universe of tomorrow. She wants ever changing architectures, creations of today, here and now; she wants each evening to be a grand evening and requires that the next evening not be the same as the festival of the evening before. She's afraid of utopia, of previsions that imprison, of routes fixed too far in advance. "It's not because I don't want things to change. On the contrary! But for me the great changes, ever dreamed and never attained, don't change a thing. It's phony to want the definitive, to want a radical change, an ideal city; it's to believe that we are masters of the world and of its environs, princes of the future. Moronic! No, I don't want that. I reject totalizing declamations because they mislead us about what we can do today, right where we are, here and now." Valerie applies this strategy to the political plane. And, first of all, to the world plane. "I'm totally committed to the Third World. I've got a boyfriend who worked in a Third World country as an alternative to military service. We used to have long discussions on the subject. Of what use have been all the plans drawn up by the technocrats of the rich countries to aid the poorer ones? Of no use whatsoever. The poor countries must be allowed to get by on their own with modest means. But they're not permitted to liberate themselves; they're aided and plundered: two ways of keeping them in servitude. I'm for today, and for micro-realizations today: a well in Sahel, for example." She has some files and some figures on that: "In 1960 the FAO conducted a world census and it discovered that 2.5% of landed proprietors control three-quarters of the arable lands in the world and that 0.23% of them control half! I read all of René Dumont's books that I can get my hands on. The agro-alimentary multinationals are reaping bonanzas—in 1974 the developing countries had to pay five times more for fertilizer than was the case three years earlier. This beats the increase in oil prices by far. Food has become a weapon in the hands of rich nations."

Obviously Valerie, who is for today and the solutions of today, is a universalist. She doesn't understand nationalism, or racism. For her a human being is a human being. Period. The skin, the ethnic origin, matter not a whit to her. And on this point she is very touchy. She roars the moment she senses the least "trace of labelling" that surfaces in the conversation of her parents who, nevertheless, she avers, are open-minded and a decent sort. "That Argentine," says her father in order to fulminate against Videla. She is just as much opposed to Videla's politics but she speaks of Argentines, she makes distinctions. She's mistrustful of any identity card, of any definition. If she hears "Arab" or "Jew" she pricks up her

ears, she takes exception to ways of speech that subsume
someone in a greater whole, that deprive him or her of par-
ticularity. She has even developed a definite taste for "individuals" to defend them against attempts at wholesale in-
clusion. She has a Breton girlfriend and she has often told her
that she can't understand why she doesn't speak Breton. Cen-
tralizations, Jacobonisms, straitjackets, make her hackles
rise. She's in favor of all political self-determinations, even of
self-management which in her view go together. For her, self-
management is to be able to live her creativity in her very
work, to react against the idea that the bankers would be the
only creators in an enterprise. For her the workers, the
engineers, the technicians are cooperators jointly engaged in
the same work. "Hierarchy" won't hold water in the face of
this necessary cooperation. All have the right to sign the work
because it's a common work. "I know a worker who's in a
big plant. Outside of his job he does primitive painting, just
like that, not from the money point of view, but as an expression of his zest for life. That's fine, of course, but it's not
normal that his workplace shouldn't permit him to be happy
when he's on the job."

Obviously, we are in full utopia here. But it is no longer the
same as the one projected by Thomas More with its avowed
purpose to solve the problems of societal life as a whole.
Valerie lives another utopia. She often uses phrases like
"bursting forth" and "exploding." She has no intention of
rationalizing society, already over-technocratized. On the
contrary, she has the desire to seek elsewhere. "Work and the
TV, everything is organized. There's no place where one can
talk. I want to participate in a space where one talks, where
one bursts forth, where one lives intensely in the fleeting moment. Like the people and situations that pop up in comic
strip balloons. That's what I mean by bursting forth, exploding, creating. In the past the great creators were those who
made a great discovery. Now they are those who can bring

about communicative relations. What's most important is to have many real friends who invent new ways of being together, of knowing how to maintain contact no matter where, and of being immediately 'open,' straight with each other, 'joined' together. I believe that people who take a joint do so because smoking together 'joins' them, they're trying to find the explosion, the bursting forth of a shared friendship. I'm in favor of small groups which are like new families. Actually, that's where I feel most at home."

If you tell Valerie that a society can not exist without institutions, she will agree. "There are structures in primitive societies, of course. But the social organization is very flexible. It's the history of these societies in which there are chiefs but in which they have no say. In a community that I know—it's a group that's a kind of tribe, and everybody gets along well with everybody else. Sure, there's a chief, but this chief is accepted by everybody and he remains a chief by common accord because, more than the others, he works for the group while respecting the freedom of each one. And the chief can always be changed. He doesn't have power in the classic sense because he doesn't take himself too seriously and because he's sure of himself, without the need to set himself up as a leader."

But why this quest for a new family on Valerie's part? Valerie, so independent, possesses a true maturity. She has no desire whatsoever to regress by entering into a sect, or a closed group in which she would find peremptory orders and simplistic slogans. She prefers to think for herself. What interests her is the informal "side" of this space. In the life of the city, in society, in the historical situation, there are always shibboleths and laws, "totalizers," appropriations or prohibitions, interdictions and regulations. Valerie needs a space in which what is wild in her and wants to remain so can express itself. It is the space afforded by the unusual, the problematical, the mobile, the unforseen explosion, and not that of the finished, well-elaborated product. In her everyday life Valerie is on the lookout for new, original encounters, for a new and unexpected event.

It was at this point that she talked with me at length about Bob Dylan. "That fellow's a nomad. I did a dossier on him. He arrives in Greenwich Village, coming from distant Minnesota. He wants to meet his idol, an old singer, Woody Guthrie, who roamed all over the United States singing folk songs for the rejects of the American system. Woody is dying in a hospital. Bob Dylan wants to emulate him, take to the road, be like a rolling stone. It's the time in which I was born, 1960, the time when young Americans said "no" to the Establishment. And Bob Dylan's songs became hymns for hundreds of thousands of Americans who marched in Washington against the war in Vietnam. Bob cries:

> 'The times they are a-changing,
> Your sons and your daughters
> are beyond your command,
> Your old road is rapidly aging,
> Please get out of the new one,
> if you can't lend your hand.'

He, Bob, never ceased changing, advancing, a lonesome cowboy who talked non-stop about politics and love. He's 'On the Road,' like the title of Jack Kerouac's book. After Kennedy's assassination, this death that marks the moment of rupture between generations and the beginning of the great protest movements in the universities—he was disgusted with the cheap politicians. Following a motorcycle accident in 1966, Dylan was silent for years. In 1971 he went back to folk singing, to the protest song. He had always been passionately interested in the struggle of Blacks and their culture. He sings a ballad, 'George Jackson,' the murder of a black militant in his prison cell. 'Watergate.' Bob sings: 'Even the President has to take off his pants from time to time.' And he always sets out again. 'One who is not busy being born is busy dying,' he sings. And always he protests against all forms of tyranny:

> 'One has no time to choose
> when truth is dying,
> One has no time to get ready
> when the victim is there.
> No time to think.'

Valerie speaks of the song as though it were a space for her, a liberation. The Blacks of the United States have refound their African origins, their identity through music. Valerie would like women to have not only their own books, but their own folklore, their own songs. And she thinks that it is high time not only that women be accorded equality and their true place, but that women's creativity be permitted to flower. That can transform society: "The utopia of yesterday was a utopia for the purpose of regulating and regimenting everything. The utopia of today, of which women are the bearers, no longer governs everything but leaves space for existence, allows for cracks, difference, the body. My mother's of Italian stock. The Mediterranean is the cradle of the Greek and patriarchal technician societies. Daughters are guarded and locked up in order to serve later as reproducers. This is clearly proven by the story of this married Algerian woman who was kidnapped in Canada by her father. On the other hand, there are societies with a less macho culture in which the women, as among the Tuaregs, are the promoters of social relations. For a long time the men in Europe cornered the productive tasks and confined women to household chores. But there's a great re-balancing in the making. Women will be increasingly involved and in even greater numbers in tasks bearing on relations, tasks which will be of prime importance by the year 2000.''

That is a great idea entertained by Valerie: the true relation. ''Before, you understand, to have relations, or connections, meant two things: to succeed, to make money, one
had to have 'relations,' connections, a quintessential form of
prostitution. People arranged dinners in order to invite
notables, those with good jobs, just to make connections and
thereby themselves get to join the fat cats' club. The second
meaning attached to 'having relations' had a sexual connotation. Thus 'relations' was used in the plural in terms of
money and sex and you had to have a lot of the one and the
other. For me, a relation signifies having a bond with others,
gratuitously. Not for the purpose of 'using' them, not for
money, but just like that, as a good thing itself, friendship,
tenderness, encounter, without any other ulterior motive,
simply to be together for its own sake, one is like in a big
family. There's a painting that's called just that: *The Big
Family*—it is a huge bird of prey soaring above the world. I
no longer want 'the family' as this permanent danger of being
kidnapped, but a real relation with my father, with my
mother. Fortunately, I've parents with whom I can disagree,
with whom I can talk. Although this doesn't go as far as is the
case with the big family of my peers, a family in which the
surname of the other never comes up, only the first name.
The other day, I took Marc home with me. We've known
each other for two years and he's been there five or six times.
After he left, my mother, in a simulated off-handed, un-
concerned manner, so that later, no doubt, she could make
some inquiries about Marc 'should things between him and
me get serious,' asked me: 'What's his name?' 'Well, Marc.'
'Marc what?' It was impossible to satisfy her curiosity. Then
she suggested: 'Look in your address book, you must have his
phone number.' 'Yes, but it's under the name Marc.' That
just drives parents up a wall because they want to situate relations, mark them, know the pedigree. For us, all that would

kill the bond with others. You meet a likable girl, you're not a cop, so you don't ask her for her identity card."

This felt need of a "true relation" is of cardinal importance to Valerie. She reacts vigorously against theories and pronouncements that promise a perfect society and she wants a real equality, one that is immediately established. "You know, I saw a poem by a youngster on democracy, in *Brèche*:

> 'Words that miscarry
> Stale words
> Democrats
> Democracies
> Words, words, and more words.'

He's right to write that. One is always using words. The French Revolution pronounced some great words on democracy and it gave birth to a society of proprietors. So many people now prattle about 'fraternity'—and, anyway, I mistrust those who mouth that word because they're often the quickest to peddle their wares to you and to try to recruit you in their ranks. For me, fraternity is not using the familiar 'you,' condescendingly, with an Arab, but using the familiar 'you' instead of the formal 'you' with each and everyone, with each and everyone I meet, with you, with the other 'even if I've seen them only once,' as a poet has put it."

Valerie's tone had become impassioned.

"You understand, I'm against all labels, the labels that are pinned on the backs of prisoners, of dissidents, of prostitutes, of foreign workers. Just the other day I was fuming against a newspaper that I'm actually quite fond of: it had been basely anti-clerical. That to me is racism. I often think of labels. I'm going to try to be very alert on this score. I don't want to judge, I don't want to pin labels. The other day I had a run-in with a girlfriend because she said, 'She's a Lesbian' about another girl. I can't stand it when a definition is pinned on anyone's back, with all due and definite norms. I find it tiresome to be provided with ready-made moulds, recipes. Life is a destiny that is ever in the making, every day. A cop can be a gangster tomorrow, and a prostitute can from this very day onwards be a friend ready to do anything in order to help someone. We're a mixture of all people, with the good and the bad. How is it possible to take people for exclusive merchandise, with catalogues, inventories, prices, wrappings?''

We laughed together over her fiery outburst. She continued along the same line.

"Nor do I understand all these adults who manage to form an instant, cocksure, definitive opinion on an event. One could say that they already know in advance what they are expected to think of all that which is happening. This is like pinning labels. And since nowadays many people feel lost, this just makes them all the more opinionated and assertive and they immediately fall in lock step with prejudices, with pre-established slogans.''

"But what do you believe in, Valerie?''

"That's it. I believe, precisely, in friendship. Being happy is to love others, to communicate with them. And the society that I want is a society that will recognize the right of each one fully to live his or her life. There's one word that I don't like, 'altruism.' In my book altruists are people who want to protectively bend over others all the time. I can't imagine bigger or more bothersome pests! To love others is at the same time also to love oneself, not to neglect oneself, not to withdraw oneself from the circuit: therefore, it's a way of bursting out, or exploring with your health, it's the capacity to do something thoroughly, to go to the limit of your resources laughing, it's having a good 'explosion,' experiencing a terrific 'intensity' in what you're doing. I want to think for myself, to experiment, to cast my imaginative capacities ever farther, to reappropriate my life. I love live, I believe in life. I believe that there are immense accumulated riches which could largely suffice for all human beings without some of them being fearful and feeling obliged to selfishly store up paintings, culture, objects, beaches and forests for themselves alone. And I believe in the future, even if there's a menace of death hanging over all humankind and its global destiny. I believe that people will succeed in positioning a process of humanization so that we can emerge from our barbarism, from the present state of our planet of which, by the way, reflective adults ought not to be inordinately proud!''

A Change of Mentality

Everyone knows at least one Valerie. But we must ask ourselves whether it is a question merely involving individual transformations, or whether something else calls for our consideration.

Is there a change of mentality? Are we really living in an era of mutation? Many acknowledge that numerous transformations have transpired in the past twenty years. But they stoutly resist the notion of mutation. They base themselves on the argument that man is ever the same with his passions and his weaknesses, his greatness and his follies. They think that young people are going through a crisis of adolescence—as they themselves had experienced it earlier—consisting of opposition to parents, but that, eventually, they will adopt a conception of life not unlike that of their progenitors. Agreed, we can call it "conflict," but it will go no further than a change of vocabulary. So it's really not worth agonizing over.

Nevertheless, we must talk of mutation, even if this perspective may astonish or displease us. It seems to be a sure fact from now on in. If we compare our epoch to the mutation that was effected at the time of the Renaissance we can, in fact, discern the same signs today. In the Renaissance a new space was given to European man: America, whose existence he had not in the slightest suspected. At that time he discovered a new world, with its customs and its riches and, by degrees, he implanted himself there, the Latins in the south, the Anglo-Saxons in the north. This new world upset his habits of thought and life. Likewise did the discovery, after centuries of Christianity, of a more profound past: paganism. Michelangelo and the Popes of the Renaissance are marked by the long-forgotten Greek paganism. The repercussions of this paganism on the mores and even on the structures of society were to be of a profound character: the Greek idea of democracy and the ideas of freedom, little by little, were to make headway in the face of Catholic monarchism. Finally, beyond a new dimension of space and a new dimension of time, a third tool of mutation was to spring up in this same epoch: Gutenberg. The printing press was to give a new dimension to the diffusion and the communication of ideas. We are the immediate witnesses to the existence of these same factors of mutation. A new dimension of space has come into permanent being: for the past twenty years science, in all spheres, has opened up prodigious new prospects to man, heralded above all by the brilliant but shattering advances in the fields of biology and of physics. Time, in other respects, has contracted. It, too, has acquired another dimension. Modern man, for example, is greatly excited over the most ancient societies discovered in the last decades and he has interested himself in their structures. Modern man fastens onto his past. Historians who recall the shattered hopes are the pet aversions of totalitarian states and of ideologists. Man is more aware now that the memory of man is of an immense importance. And the powers that be, those that hold the present in their hands, try to appropriate the past to themselves, because they are familiar with what George Orwell wrote in *1984:* "He who controls the past controls the future. He who controls the present controls the past." Time, henceforth, is also confronted with speed: "Speed," writes Paul Virilio in *Vitesse et Politique [Speed and Politics]*[1] "suddenly equals the annihilation of time: it is the state of emergency." And the perfection of the engines of war bears first of all on their rapidity of intervention. The industrial revolution of the last century imposed the railroad train, a technological vehicle. Before that, man was an integral part of the horse and traversed all terrains. Then the train imposed its own infrastructure, its rails, and adapted the environment to its own ends. It was the same with the automobile and the resultant network of highways. This is how we have arrived at the desire ceaselessly to fight against time, to gain time. Now, although we can achieve a certain direct mastery over space, this is not possible with time. It's an illusion to believe that one has "gained" time. Even though one may have accomplished a journey more quickly, the question of the utilization of the whole of time remains always there. Modern man is decentered from time: speed gives him idle periods which often he doesn't know what to do with. And the accelerated automation which will reduce labor time will pose the question of the human employment of time even further. Modern man can no longer peaceably follow the course of the seasons, the ancestral rhythms, and he is dangerously subjected to repetitiousness, to standardization in his tasks and in his leisure time. He knows that in order to escape this danger, from now onwards, he must create a new manner of living time.

In the service of this new space and this new time we now have electronics, infinitely more efficient than Gutenberg. The computer has permitted science to surmount summits hitherto inaccessible. It permits the ruling powers to control the present as it has never been controlled before. It can also permit a new everyday freedom.

Hence we can say that the man of today is living in an era

of mutation. But at the same time this mutation is marked by a radical novelty on which we must dwell. This novelty is that of the possibility—and one that henceforth can be believed as certain—of the total death of all human beings, of all humankind. Today all States have in their hands the wherewithal that can reduce the planet of man and the whole history of man to nothingness. It is not an apocalyptic vision, a pessimistic prophetism: it is a fact as rigorous as the assertion that two and two make four. Never has the world known such a possibility. War, pestilence, famine hitherto could exterminate millions of human beings. Today's atomic and chemical weapons can destroy all life on earth. This menace, the demographic problem and the Third World are the burning questions of our time. These questions are not of a local character, but questions of world scope. They are not accidental questions, but a question of life and death. It is necessary for us to realize why so much has been written on death for the past ten years. It's because this perspective of the possibility of a death—no longer that of some human beings, but that of the human species as such—is by degrees penetrating the consciousness of our contemporaries. Savants, intellectuals were the first to acquire this awareness which gradually is being extended to the whole human population. This perspective is being resisted by those who are less young, those who have acquired a carapace and think that the world will always get itself out of this fix somehow. Such people have adopted an ostrich-like policy and live by rote. But there is also an increasing number of people who are tending to look this "monster" in the face. This shark comes from the bottommost depths of the sea and is called Annihilation. The fact is that the men of power and of the entertainment world try to amuse the man of today and to divert his attention from this view, and to make him glimpse "solutions" come from "elsewhere," "encounters of a third type" which will bring peace and life to earth. But these multiple diversions merely highlight the reality and the acuteness of the problem.

Hence we are decidedly in an era of mutation, and the mutation is effected most particularly in the "western" world—it would be more proper perhaps to say the "northern" world because it involves an ensemble of territories stretching from California to Japan, and across the Atlantic, Europe to the Urals. Even though the Soviet sphere, in part, escapes this storm because it has certain means to hide it, the fact remains that it itself is being buffeted by it. But here we shall more particularly be discussing the "western" world as distinct from the countries of the East, of which countries like Italy, Germany, France, Belgium, in short the countries that constitute the Common Market, form a part.

It Must Be Seen To Be Believed

No one will challenge the assertion that this "western" world is, accordingly, a zone of turbulence: instead of imperturbably pursuing its route the plane is being tossed about, it fails to respond to the orders of the pilot. The western cultural system, from now onwards, is unstable, it no longer functions as before, it fears for its skin, it's afraid of being absorbed by a black hole of sorts, as mysterious as the Bermuda triangle. Yet a cultural system is a possibility of communication, a language, an ensemble of signs through which men establish bonds between one another, trying to tell each other, according to their respective lights, just what life and death, violence and love are all about.

Before, it was easy to take one's bearings and to recover one's course; before, it was easy to "believe"—in the broadest sense of the term. Today the reference points have become blurred, one gets lost in them, there are no guide marks, no havens in which to take shelter. This begets a total bewilderment and has put an end to peremptoriness. The resultant permissiveness yields an extreme relativism and each one feels endangered in the face of the risk of finding oneself in the face of a calamity of whatever kind. Each one tries to find one's own identity, to acquire a true personality, but it is only with difficulty that one arrives at it. The perturbation is global.

These are not, of course, simply metaphors. The turbulence in which the cultural system finds itself caught up is best expressed by viewing it in terms of the status of an orphan: a new world is trying to discover itself and perceives right off that it has no father. Thenceforth for this fatherless world it becomes a matter, autodidactically, of proposing new projects to oneself and a new way to live. Being orphaned is deeply traumatizing, above all when such a status here no longer applies to some individuals who, having lost a father, can nevertheless find some substitutes, but to an ensemble, to a massive group. Now it is an entire world, in the West, that feels orphaned, deprived of any reference to a cultural system that preceded it, a world composed above all, but not solely, of what has been called "the black continent," the young, the women, the marginalized. This world is in fact shrouded in darkness: it has no compass or compass-card with which to guide itself, no father image that leads the way to mark out the route. Hence the very fact of this absence of assured guide marks leads in our time to an enormous difficulty in the matter of "believing." Believing is attaching oneself to a star that we take as a reference mark for our route. But if we arrive at thinking that there is no star capable of truly orienting us, that the stars are multiple, contradictory, relative to each other, we can no longer "believe." Several years back a certain number of those who are called "unbelievers" expressed their irritation, and rightly so, at being tagged with such a negative term. And to their protest they added that they did believe in something. Often, moreover, they were militants, generous souls, unflaggingly vowed to a cause, to a movement, to a party. Although they have convictions other than the Christian faith, they were convictions nevertheless and as strong as Christian faith, certitudes to which they gave their faith, their fidelity, their acts.

Today, matters of faith—whatever this faith may be—are much more difficult to deal with. The abbé de L'Epée, who died in 1789, devoted his whole life to the education of deaf-mutes, as is known. He had noted that the verb "to believe" was one of the most impossible for his pupils to grasp, and he explained: "Here is the way I proceed in order to succeed. After writing *I believe* on the blackboard, I draw four different lines arranged as follows:

I believe
$$\begin{cases} \text{I say } yes \text{ with the mind; I think } yes \\ \text{I say } yes \text{ with the heart; I love to think } yes \\ \text{I say } yes \text{ with the mouth} \\ \text{I do not see with my eyes.} \end{cases}$$

"Which means: my mind consents, my heart adheres, my mouth professes, but I don't at all see with my eyes. Once it is thus explained my pupils understand this word much more than do those who can talk and hear."

But the problem today lies precisely in the fact that we, men and women, have been habituated to give a radically preferential right to *seeing.* for us seeing is believing. Thus abbé de L'Epée's four propositions are absolutely reversed. Modern man cannot say *yes* with the mind, the heart and the mouth before having *seen.* Hence he cannot arrive at believing. Modern man has a need to see, to ascertain visible, sure, proved things. Science arrived in the last century and along with it positivism. The experimental method is the universal, predominant method of our epoch, scientific culture, triumphantly in process of globalization, has imposed itself everywhere, without wars and through wars. A century ago, in 1875, one could read the following in the *Grand Larousse:* "Science always carefully reserves the freedom to judge and to choose. Faith always gives a single, authoritarian, tyrannical solution . . . Hence faith does not provide any solution to great problems save to minds that have decided to make no further effort to resolve them" (article, *Science*). For a century science has foisted its methods on us and in view of its prestige, in view of its rigor and efficacy, many have judged philosophy to be an archaic knowledge, tainted with subjectivism as attested by the multiplicity of its tendencies. But at the same time this infatuation with science has produced, on occasion, a triumphalism and even a kind of dogmatism, if not sectarianism. Thus we are witnessing, paradoxically, in our day a suppleness in philosophy which, formerly accused of proceeding from a *petitio principii,* a begging of the question, and of affirming certitude from on high, today increasingly cultivates doubt. As a result, some are infusing into science a will to dominate everything, asserting that science gives an index of total credibility, to the point that there is an ever increasing reaction to this methodological imperialism which "impairs all work of research and of deepening elaboration."[2]

Thus today we find ourselves facing the dual attitude of our contemporaries toward science: many among them believe with an iron-clad faith in a certain number of things because they believe that science gathers all together and solves all. On the other hand, a small number, and among them we find first of all true scientists, underscore that science operates within limits, that it determines only what it renders determinable, that it remains ceaselessly open and reformable. But, alongside these scientists there are ideologues who use the magic word "science" in order to have their message pass as scientific, that is, as something that man can view as sure and absolute. For example, on

June 25, 1978, TV viewers could hear Jeannette Thorez-Vermeersch declare her faith in communism not only with the air of sureness that two and two make four, but even that two and two make five. This for the reason that communism assertedly is scientific and therefore truth. And there are also the technicians who utilize science in an apparently objective manner but who, in fact, avail themselves of its applications in order to foist, by procedures that are alike everywhere, a setting for the exploitation of the entire world. The multinational corporations are the pure product of this technico-scientific culture which produces economic, administrative and political rationalization and which, in all countries, brings about a generalization of a certain urbanized life-style, of uniformization of mentalities and tastes, of dress and of leisure, of languages and of behavior. In such a context, it's difficult to believe. One becomes a fatalist: "This is the situation that prevails, science has spoken, all we can do is bow. It's ineluctable." These are the *eyes*, these are the ascertained proofs on which the decision is based. The imperialism of *seeing* is encroaching everywhere, everything is ascribed to *seeing,* and everything imposes itself through sight. One says: "It's objective" and all one can do is say *amen* and acquiesce. Everything is submitted to the criterion of the camera, of the lens—that which lies before the eye, that which is attained through sight, and that which appears as evident.

History Of A Resistance

This conquest of the planet by seeing and technique was effected most particularly from World War II onwards. In 1945 the whole of the western world—the USSR and Japan included—had made an immense leap forward as regards scientific and technical discoveries. The explosion of consumer goods and conveniences has given rise to a kind of new man:

a technician and a robotized man, the product of the radio, cinema and television, and interested first and foremost in everyday utensils and gadgets like vacuum cleaners, washing machines and, in general, in the means for making everything impeccable and sleek. The universe was thus promised to man as a sanitized, medicalized universe, finally rid of diseases and blemishes, including mosquitoes and other bothersome insects that DDT and its derivatives, so it was thought, would rapidly exterminate. Everything was going to be imperturbably rationalized. And high-rises with their umpteen stories, their clear, spotless walls and their glass facades were to replace the old houses that had been banged together in some way or other and were situated on narrow, tortuous streets. Everything was to be regulated. Such was the perspective of the years 1945-1960.

The year 1960 saw the birth of a reaction in the face of this immense rationalization, a reaction proportioned to the serried straitjacketing in which a certain "civilization"—but can this universal sameness be called a civilization?—wanted to fence man.

Those who reacted could not be the men and women who had, almost irremediably, been de-natured by this "civilization" and who lost themselves in the ceaseless search for consumer goods and who had been captured by the mail order catalogues or the supermarkets. Such people remain bogged down in budgeting and abundance. And they did not see, from the depths of their limited materialist abyss, what other salvation there might be to wish for. They accepted the routine job and the subway in order to achieve an agreeable nirvana: job, home, bed. In other words, the repetitiousness that relieves us from care and from creativeness, the reiteration of the past, and from sleep as a primary rhythm.

It's easy, today, twenty years later to describe this *homo* who sought above all for a certain repose and the absence of adventures. For the reason that we have been able to step backward and from this perspective we can perceive the dehumanization to which such a conception of life fatally leads. But it is not so clear for those who, after the harsh vicissitudes of the war and the efforts to achieve a new growth in the first fifteen years of the post-war period, found facing them the whole range of those objects which appeared to them like a new world, a promised land. To be fifty years old—or even simply thirty—in 1960 was to have known at first hand the convulsions of a world enveloped in flames and soaked in blood. It was tempting to seek forgetfulness and repose.

We can understand why the best sociologists predicted in 1960 a new era: thus, for example, Roderich Sridenberg who, in his *Posthistoric Man* foresaw for the future an increasingly uniformed culture, tailored to the measure of techniques everywhere alike.

That this culture has mightily foisted itself on us is a fact of which we are inescapably aware, and it continues to invade the world. It appears that it is bound to increasingly efface "believing" of its certitudes to the advantage of "seeing." Nevertheless the beginning of 1960, almost everywhere in the western world, witnessed a raising of shields, a revolt against this uniformized culture that its proponents wanted surreptitiously to foist on the world.

But, among the populations of the West, who was it that reacted, from 1960 onwards, against the automatization of behavior, which began to force itself on us in a manner that was at once sly and brutal? It was first of all the young generation, those under twenty, those who had not known the war and who, on the other hand, had imbibed, almost with their mother's milk, the delights of abundance. Their parents had known hunger and fear, but they had developed at the pace of young gods unbeset by fear and problems, in the tread of the global growth of the West. It was not only bread that they had eaten to the point of satiety, it was cake.

But if such was the case, why the revolt among such a great number of them from California to Japan by way of New York, London or Berlin? It will be objected: man does not live by bread alone and by cinema—*panem et circenses*—even less by cake and television. Yes, this youth of 1960 and those that followed them wanted an "elsewhere", an "otherness." The real and the rational did not suffice them, they wanted the stuff of dreams. Of dreams and of the relational. Seated like little princes on the treasures piled up by their parents, they had a presentiment that this accumulated money and progress were distancing them from a whole part of the planet, from India to Latin America, from Africa to Vietnam, which was growing ever poorer but which still wanted to elevate itself through freedom. In the very measure in which they were becoming affluent, young westerners perceived that they were losing the sense of being and the sense of the other. French or North Americans, they did not want to colonize the young people of Vietnam or of Africa but, rather, to learn from them another way of life. And their ethnologists—Claude Lévi-Strauss or Margaret Mead—began to make them discover that these territories contained resources other than minerals, namely uncommon and utterly fascinating societies and human beings.

From 1960 onwards, a certain monolithic culture, based on the presumed scientific certitudes was shaken, battered by a small number of human beings: young people and women who instinctively reacted against them, but also critics, artists, scientists. The latter, for example, noted that 1945 was the date of the explosion of the production of consumer goods as well as the year of Hiroshima, the year in which a disastrous scientific application had shown that although science is an admirable success, it cannot act alone. Thereupon dawned the realization that there can be no culture according to science alone, that left to itself science, through cold technology incurs, almost ineluctably, the risk of leading humankind to total catastrophe; that scientific research is itself implanted in a social life and that, without sufficient reflection, science leads to the temptation of direct action, of extreme violence. How could we not see here the monsters who utilize psychiatric discoveries for political ends? From 1960 onwards, savants, artists, mystics, while duly recognizing science, reacted in the name of a creative battle for mankind and denounced totalitarian forms of knowledge and power.

Thus the culture of *seeing,* which laid claim to universal recognition, had its wings clipped from 1960 onwards and the clipping operation has continued even further in the course of the last years. But it must be clearly perceived that the culture of seeing remains a mastodon that seduces the masses and that quests for another type of culture are embryonic, difficult.

In the face of this imposing culture of seeing, the first resistance actions were of a confining character: from 1960 onwards the first hippies, for example, opposed this culture by rejecting, purely and simply, science and modernity. They tried to reproduce old models of life, deeming that this archaism and this return to the past sufficed to meet the needs of the future. At the same time they wanted to revive particular cultures, ethnicities, folklores, rites, all that which is essentially subject to the erosion effected by the irresistibly globalizing and universalizing culture of "seeing". And "looking backward" became a taste, a fashion, a quest. These different ways of protecting oneself against the culture of "seeing" were all manifestations of resistance to this culture and they asserted that there was not only the "rational" or the "obvious." Another dimension, which had been repressed by the passion for scientificity, began to reappear with great force: the irrational, the elsewhere, the different.

The irruption of the irrational, moreover, was fostered by

the "human sciences" whose rise dates from 1960 onwards. In the last century, with Darwin, man had discovered himself as a participant in a long chain of animal species. But, thanks to science, it was he who had discovered it and from that moment onwards he could place himself at the summit of evolution. With the advent of psychoanalysis, however, man discovers himself to be similar to an iceberg of which he knows only the tip and nothing whatsoever about the immense part submerged in the depths. Man's consciousness then see-saws, and it cannot tell itself whether it knows everything and whether it can do everything. Man, who from time immemorial, knows himself to be mortal, today also knows that within him there is an unknown zone, as terrifying as death, a depth that eludes him.

Before, it was the scientific certitudes that made it difficult "to believe". To them there has now been added the immense abyssal ocean of uncertainties that make man suspicious of choices and acts which he formerly believed to be free and sovereign. Thus, a new—and terrible—difficulty blocks the road to "believing". For it is from the very heart of his act of faith, and no longer from outside conflict, that the man of today asks himself whether he truly believes what he believes, whether his act of faith may not be commanded by unsuspected, unconscious imperatives. Previously, it was "seeing" that had attacked "believing" and had put it on the defensive. Today it too and, above all, many non-evident matters challenge "belief." Even staunch believers, those who unconditionally follow an ideology or a cause, militants for whom without the bat of an eyelash we should proceed from *seeing* to "judging" and "acting", even these people are on a collision course with their children for whom "seeing" is just not that evident, for whom the essential work consists first of all in mistrusting "seeing" as if it was an optical illusion.

Many adults are astonished to see many young people, and

even some not so young, in numbers beyond counting, who are in this condition and who are nevertheless very credulous about phenomena lacking substantial proof: UFO's for example. Is there a contradiction?

The reaction against a prison-like universe erected around modern man by the straitjacket of production, of technique, of information, of advertising, has manifested itself in a recourse to the irrational, to the imagination. The desire to invent something else, to be otherwise, the need to wander along the roads of utopia and, accordingly, to question pre-established models and schema is a necessity today for those who are vigilant: the world right now needs prospectors of the future who, without entirely neglecting the givens, the discoveries and the scientific methods, try to extricate the world from this centralist technocracy in which it risks being fenced. And only this kind of inventiveness can help us avoid violence. For a society that has succeeded technically but which is life-crushing does not flower beyond formal organization and the stabilization of order: it begets boredom, disgust with living, soon followed by madness no matter of what kind. A minority of our contemporaries, young and not so young, has understood this compelling need of creativity, a creativity not immediately individual but collective, in which men and women will escape the dreary destiny of an ever repeated sameness in order to make place for multiple sudden appearances of self-management and creative acts. Basing themselves on science and its methods, appraising the prodigious perspectives that it opens, this minority is trying to pair realism and the irrational, for the sake of humanity's future.

Components Of This New Mentality

Here we should like to describe in detail this new mentality, a blend of scientific knowledge and utopian passion, this mentality which, at one and the same time, concentrates in itself a habit of believing only what it sees and an attitude of openness towards the zaniest and the most non-evident perspectives.

But before all else it must once more be underscored that the menality, in which science and fiction blend and conform to each other, is new. In the humanist culture in which "the man of honor" reproduces and transmits a wisdom and a truth handed down from generation to generation, it is hardly a question of using one's imagination in order to change the transmitted wisdom and precepts. In the scientific culture, which tends to make of science an idol, one is also passive in the face of what has been newly discovered with a kind of interdict that prevents a re-questioning of the validity of the earlier discovery.

Now, since 1946, western humanists have been more adept in discovering that there were scores of other wisdoms, as fitted to aid man to live as their own. And many children of these humanists have begun to study these other wisdoms, particularly those of Asia. In other respects, the extraordinary acceleration of contemporary discoveries has obliged scientists to give more and more evidence of imagination, to go constantly beyond the theories seemingly accepted by others, rendering them even more extraordinary.

For some time now men have succeeded in launching objects into the atmosphere which, at a certain moment, escape terrestrial gravitation. Likewise, a certain mentality has sprung up, acquired its autonomy and also detached itself from the terrestrial gravitation that had seemed absolutely inescapable, namely from the conventional wisdoms and from the established sciences.

"Believing" is based most particularly on what has been transmitted. Christians, for example, take the faith of the apostles for a base, a faith that is followed from generation to generation. Those who believe in this or that wisdom do likewise. But those who believe in science as in a store of knowledge that has been accumulated by those who have preceded us and that has already permitted—and will permit—an updating of the secrets of life and better living conditions also operate in the order of "believing".

At the same time, "believing" offers the perspective of a "beyond", of an elsewhere, be it a heaven, or be it singing tomorrows. But this sky and these tomorrows, if they are evoked poetically, appear as other worlds that cannot be absolutely described in a precise fashion.

"Believing" is thus moored to a past which keeps it closely alongside the dock of history. And if phantasms of a "down-there", of a far away place, of a great open space develop, these are objects of faith and not possible creations of man himself.

Now our analysis shows clearly that with the new mentality there is combined in an explosive mixture the strictest seeing and zaniest imagining, seeing is a present reality that is opposed to the past or that takes no account of it save to "go beyond it", and that the imaginary is a reality that is also present in the sense that it involves rendering present and real, solely through the forces of man, the boldest imaginations and the most extravagant hopes. Through a twofold movement, the new mentality escapes terrestrial gravitation—that of the past—and it rejects celestial gravitation by wanting to create a heaven on earth.

We see that thus "believing" has become quite difficult for someone who belongs to this advanced culture which is the new mentality. And that Christian faith and hope, such as they appear, such as they are in fact lived by a good number of Christians, seem realities that take on a folkloric and phantasmagoric character at one and the same time.

But some may object that "this talk of the new mentality being dunned into our ears is quite debatable." Let us suppose that it is only an hypothesis, but an hypothesis is always a wager on the future. An hypothesis always makes the future happen sooner, even if it proves inexact. For it has prompted reflection. There would have been no science had it not been for the boldness of a certain number of men who, using the experimental method, posed hypotheses. The same applies to art. To refuse to consider an hypothesis *a priori* or to reject it emotionally is to be stagnant. On the other hand, this hypothesis is not so zany or far-fetched: "They are not primarily ideas that had assertedly been elaborated, lucubrated by armchair strategists. Ideas do not guide the world to such an extent; they are born with history and human freedom, they do not fall from on high. It was not Marcuse who brought into being May '68. Rather, it was a general movement, at the level, moreover, of our whole planet, a movement which began approximately a century before and which exploded around 1960 after a slow, long journey. It is this movement that begot May '68 which, therefore, cannot be viewed as a spontaneous generation.

And we must clearly see that some who wish to reject this new mentality do so because of their own well-established ideology or for the sake of their entrenched positions. Even if a majority does not live this mentality, each year it is increasingly influenced and impregnated by it. This "other" mentality, different from that which is lived by the majority of modern people, nevertheless exists in a diffused way in this very majority which receives a real influence from it. But it takes root more particularly in two groups of the population, the "bio-social" groups, namely young people and women. Young people, perhaps because of their numbers but above all because of the global evolution of the world, have become aware in a massive way of the fact that the principles that guided adults have hardly brought justice and peace to the world and that therefore there must have been something decrepit and decaying about them. Women have acquired the same awareness: they have perceived that the principles that guided men (their husbands, their fathers, their brothers) were of slight efficacy as regards the planet's future. Thus young people and women began to contest the "culture" that preponderantly governed the world. It is a muted contestation, but one that runs very deep because it is vital.

At the same time we can see that what is at issue here is something altogether different from a protest, a demand. Young people and women clearly feel that if they limit themselves exclusively to a demand to share the power of adults and males and that if they struggle only in order to appropriate this power, they are but recognizing the cogency, the merits of this power as it is, and viewing the power holders in a positive sense. Thus they would merely be the accomplices of adult and male power.

They do not want merely to have increasing access to adult male power or to see to it that this power changes hands. They go much further: their heart-felt desire is that no human being should have a power over another human being, whoever he or she may be. They want to empty "authority" of its power of death, of alienation over others. They view the world of adults and males as a world of conquest, of violence, of colonization, of machismo, of aggression. The values that they advocate are of another order: non-violence, compassion, tenderness, the taste for happiness and for beauty, disappropriation, peace, brotherhood.

These participants in the "new mentality" do not place themselves outside the world. They do not set themselves up alongside the great star Sirius, on a lofty height, like angels who would wash their hands (angels have no hands!) of the vicissitudes, the "nightmare of history" like beings who extricate themselves from it through flight. They are of the opinion that nobody has a knowledge of such a kind that radically transcends that of others; that there is no global political response that can lead ineluctably to a golden age, to a good and perfect society; that it is necessary to struggle without let-up so that all power and authority remain relative and are not travestied into an absolute for which its holders ever hanker. They know that it's very hard work to dedicate oneself to a future ever in the making, with an unremitting lucidity because the work is never really over.

Two components above all seem to permit them to resist the assaults of the previous mentalities and which are still gloriously regnant today—and which, moreover, do everything they can to reduce or even to wipe out this new mentality, proof that they fear it.

The first component is a fact-mindedness. Those who participate in this "new mentality" have an altogether particular fact-mindedness. They have been formed, as a matter of fact, by experimental methods and they have had to confront the everyday experience of existence more than others. They are closer to nature and to life, less subject to dangerous radiations of abstractions, they are more pragmatic and concrete. Moreover, they inform themselves on an enormous scale, and with knowledge taken from real life. They have a passion for understanding and knowing what blasé old campaigners who are so sure they know everything, thanks to their principles, have lost even before learning it. It's a new, fresh world, uncultivated, full of possibilities, that's standing out there.

The second component is creative-affectivity. The preceding mentalities were strongly characterized by a rigorous dualism: the body and the soul, the temporal and the spiritual, with emphasis on the latter, on the noble values, the soul, the mind considered as superior to the other powers of mankind. Even today there is a way of according a privileged status to the ideology that still exhibits a dualism: the ideology is placed at the pinnacle and the self-management of everyday life is viewed as secondary, as corollary. There is also another dualism: work and leisure. On the one hand our society foists work with its rigid rationalization and functionalization; on the other, it foists (cunningly, but effectively) excitants such as a TV set that hisses psst!, second-hand musical and sport events, tawdry adventures. And therein lies a duality, a new cleavage of the human being.

The participants of the "new mentality" rise in revolt against this state of affairs. They want a "qualitative" work, a work capable of making man flower and of effecting his self-realization. They want a creative leisure time that does not moronize man but, instead, offers him feasts, celebrations, in which he will know the joy of existence, of being himself and of being in communication with others. They want a unity of life in which leisure and work can be harmonized. They want cities tailored to human measure which are not dormitories inhabited by men and women condemned to "atomizing" tasks, that is, to tasks that cut one up into tiny pieces, that put one in a strait-jacket. Rather, they want cities whose dwellers build and celebrate at one and the same time.

To be sure, we can think that this new mentality, squeezed between a liberal society inspired by ancient humanism desirous of self-renewal, and a Stalinist "scientific" revolutionary ideology desirous of broadening bastions, has only slim chances of finding a breach for a breakthrough. Edgar Morin has discussed this "aspiration" to another life, to another society, to another politics, a politics "that will not be based on wooden ideas, on a wooden language, on a one-dimensional view of man and of society."

Yet for him this aspiration is ceaselessly re-born because the new generations make a round trip tour of the advanced liberal society and of the backward revolutionary ideology with an ever-increasing swiftness! And is less and less soaked up by submissive adjustments to socio-professional life, by all-purpose ideologies, by the great and outworn mythology. The fact is that this "great aspiration" "always errs", it always lets itself be mythified, even for a brief time, and "it unconsciously betrays itself by contributing to the maintenance and to the triumph of the great oppression of the century. We are always in dubious battle."[3]

If it's dubious, some will object, why dwell on the new mentality? So these princes of the past and these materialists of comprehensive insurance want to continue to express faith in the humanist culture and the assertedly scientistic culture which are well-established cultures. Yet Christ asks that his message be proclaimed first and foremost to the poor, to those not in power as are these two cultures that are at once antagonistic authorities, brother-enemies and sharers-accomplices of power. Those who belong to this new mentality know very well to what point they are "poor", being the products of the two cultures in which, nevertheless, they find themselves oppressed and which they reject. Society, of course, with its two cultures on its flanks can continue to advance and carry along with it the institutions that are fitted into one or the other of these two cultures. It can try to derail this new embryonic mentality which asks to exist not only among some who manage to resist but also on behalf of a mass of people. But this society, as Edgar Morin states, has on its flank "a breach through which the new forms, the cultural themes, the problems that were smouldering, germinating, rush in." "The breach is always open on our society's flank."[4]

And Morin employs another comparison, that of "undergrounds". To grasp this new mentality it must be seen not as a prosperous, grandiose construction but as an underground reality developing its life in the depths. "It is in the undergrounds of society, it is in the air that it breathes that something has changed, that the viruses are in full swing."[5] What does Ferreri show us in his film "Monkey's Dream"? The actor Depardieu has a job which entails attending to the wings, to the basement of a theatre, to tiny subterranean beasts such as the rats, to a pint-sized monkey issued from King-Kong's loins, to vaults, to holes and to all that which transpires in the pits of things. Why should one be afraid to dare to look at what transpires underneath the brilliant and decadent exterior of our civilization?

"How can we avoid looking for the real bottommost layer that hides under our concepts?" writes Jean Duvignaud. The mythical or symbolical systems are not intellectual constructions: they concern everyday life and undergo the variations that the latter foist on them. A permanent mutation affects the ensembles that one naively thinks of reconstructing in an inalterable, immobile perspective."[6]

Why not dare admit that there is underneath the progress and the wastes of our cultures, another mentality that is trying to be born and is not as ugly and as perilous as we are prone to believe?

In Quest Of The Present Time

The man of this end of the 20th century thinks of the third millenium. Books are published, like the one that wants to attempt a preview of "the next ten thousand years." This man has been able to succeed in dating his first ancestor—*homo sapiens*—and he has traced him back as far as fifty thousand years. This man who did not live beyond the age of thirty-two centuries ago knows that soon the advances of science will lead him easily to live up to one hundred and twenty years: often the duration of a marriage attains to but fifty years. Time seems to lengthen.

But, at the same time, man knows that his days are numbered. In the past twenty years there has existed the danger that the whole of mankind can henceforth be scratched from the rolls of existence. The world's population will have quintupled between 1930 and 2000. Hence the days allotted to man to resolve this double menace of death, by destruction or by over-population, are also numbered. In other respects, space seems to have abolished time, and the passenger who boards the Concorde in Paris will arrive in the United States earlier than his boarding time: a false and poisonous image because man pressed to gain time burns spaces, normal intervals, vital rhythms. Now man knows that he can no longer take his time, that he no longer has time to lose in order to provide for a strategy for tomorrow and to see to it that the coming years are not the apocalypse and the end of time. The future is there, present, already begun. The future is urgent. A future that it was thought would be easy to domesticate because it was unfolding, so it was thought, according to a certain linear process, according to a direction of history, whether in the capitalist direction, through the clearly perceived and well-understood interests of each one, or in the Marxist direction, through the dialectic play of the relations of production.

The young people, and some others along with them, know more and more, owing to their world consciousness in which the Third World occupies the first place, owing to their ecological perspectives, that history is no longer natural, that it does not unfold by itself, that it can shatter just like a human life, at any moment. They also consider that there is no event that can, with the wave of a magic wand, change life, create another way, paradoxically, of life. That there is no hidden certain unity of time and space in which all men will meet, communing in the same rites and the same ideals, in a perfect equality.

Consequently the participants in this new mentality want to create something different *here* and *now,* right there where they are and immediately, arguing that the tiniest daily, punctual transformation will have a greater reverberation and contagion than the great ideas of the profesisonals of change. They no longer draw up inventories of values, nor catalogues of finalities but, rather, inventories of their modest possibilities and catalogues of their present resources.

It must also be noted that those who live according to the

new mentality share the conviction that time no longer has unity, that there are all kinds of "times", of dead times and living times, of lost times and gained times. They also discover that the manner in which an adult, a professor, a board chairman lives this time is radically different from that of a young person, a monk or an African, that time is different for those who live the day and for those who live the night, different according to whether one performs an exciting or a boring job, according to whether one is a man or a woman, a mountaineer or a city dweller.

In the face of this evolution of the nature of time—time is no longer what it was—how do the bearers of the new mentality live time? For them time has become essentially an intensity: it is a matter of being present to the present. Someone who is living is not the one who says, like Dr. Faust, "Tarry awhile, thou art so fair", but one who accepts, with equanimity, that the instant dies, that time not be an everlastingness, a continuity but, rather, a succession of presents. And precisely for this reason it is an acquiescence to a series of deaths so that other intense moments may rise again. The perishable, instead of engendering melancholy, is lived as an improvisation, an explosion, as disappropriation and thus as joy. The essential point is not to collect souvenirs but, rather, to be as Nietsche says, "the child who laughs", there, in the very instant.

Accordingly there is in the new mentality an acceptance of time as a present moment in the same way as there is an acquiescence to what "is there," to the body, to rootedness, to the singular, to what one can touch today.

Over against this acquiescence to the present, we are witnessing the rebirth of a "gnostic" mentality which is the opposite of this new mentality. According to this gnostic mentality, one must extricate oneself from time and not submit to it. Time is a defilement, an exile, it is a sign of the imperfection of being, and any incarnation appears as an evil, a "slough", a "cesspool", a "prison". These "gnostics" want to alight from the train of history, escape from its paths, take refuge in far-off places where time seems abolished and to realize communities outside time with others who, like them, are unsubdued, rebels against history. They want, each one, to be an "Angel" as two young philosophers recently programmed them. They want to set aright this wicked creation, give it a guide-mark outside time and restore to the world a radiant re-beginning, sublimating everyday activities.

We can see to what point the new mentality runs into conflict on this terrain which it has chosen out of a fidelity to the present moment and out of a will to continual renewal. Its weapons of resistance are not to be found in arsenals, being weapons of an ungraspable and unrepeatable type, keen, momentary quality, such as humor and gratuitousness, qualities of the instant, the "almost nothing", the "impalpable" as W. Jankélévitch defines it. Nevertheless it also pursues a fundamental quest. This new conception of time is a boldness proper to young people, the boldness of looking death square in the face, of knowing that all being is mortal, that all love encounters death, not only sooner or later, but every day. It is no longer possible, henceforth, to establish the relation with others primarily on laws, on a contract, on a stable society. It is a matter of structuring a love knowing that it ceaselessly depends on the other, and not on guarantees, legal or of any other character. It is a matter of giving up the narcissistic quest of being loved "for always", of giving up as lost a pseudo-eternity of love in which one imprisons the other. In this new mentality one learns to live the fact that no one possessed another, that the presence of others and the presence to others always transpires against a backdrop of absence and are not based on the certitude of appropriations.

Jean Duvignaud has studied "the collective or individual activities that reveal the excess of dynamism or of vitality through which man is distinguished from the beast: symbolism, play, trance, laughter, and above all the gift. The gift which, stripped of the idea of trade or commerce . . . is indeed the better part of man."[7]

The participants in the new mentality understand Duvignaud's particular language: "To give without reason, to give whatever one is or one has. And by so doing to suppress the attachments to property or to gain, to open oneself to a bursting forth."[8] And Duvignaud can but recapitulate[9] what several have said in concert with him.[10] Casamayor, for example, or R. Gerard in his last book where he asserts that a certain idea of sacrifice is alien to Jesus' message. Jean Duvignaud protests against the "commercialization of sacrifice" according to which "the saint must win eternal life in *exchange* for the time spent in prayers."[11]

Gratuitousness, gift of little, refusal to accept the notion that time is money. And Duvignaud remarks how this act of renewal is primarily effected "by men or by women who, in other respects, possess nothing or almost nothing. It is in terms of rarity that this kind of wager on a possible change in the order of things and in the organization of society must be understood."[12]

There is an "excess of being" in man and he appears to be "the only species to possess it."[13] This dynamism full of anticipatory behaviour goes beyond routine fabrications. Doubtless it is necessary to think that the signs that indicate the existence of this new mentality show that today there is access to a stage of mutation of man and that this advance, subversive by nature, upsets established models but creates a new relation of man with others, with the world, with nature and himself.

II

THE PARTISANS OF THE NIGHT

Faith is a "spiritual combat, harsher than a battle of men," as Rimbaud had already clearly seen. A combat against what? Against unbelief, tenacious unbelief that ever surfaces afresh. To present faith as a reality that stands to reason is a deceit, if not an imposture. To deem, as Christians have done all too often, that one who does not believe in the existence of God immediately denies the evidence of the senses and that his intelligence, accordingly, is not up to par, is to display lots of pretentiousness and precipitancy. The great mystics, from Teresa of Avila to Thérèse of Lisieux, from John of the Cross to Charles de Foucauld, have lived their profoundest faith in the night. Charles de Foucauld wrote about it to Louis Massignon on July 15, six months before his death: "As for Jesus' love for us, he has proved it clearly enough for us to believe in it without being able to feel it. To feel we loved him and he loves us would be heaven. But heaven is not, except at rare moments and in rare cases, for us here below."[1]

The Night of Believers

Well known is the admirable prayer of St. John of the Cross in which he sings that he lives the faith. But "on a dark night."

Thérèse of Lisieux also knows "darkness," real "darkness." But there is nothing morbid about it: "She has too much of a taste for the happiness of faith, on this earth, to feel the slightest attraction for false morbid sufferings or to create puerile crises for herself in which the soul nourishes itself on its states of soul. There is one fact that this little woman of Normandy, a very concrete personality, particular-

ly notes: she enjoys a feeling of happiness, then she no longer
experiences it. Never had she sought the mortifications and
disciplines that most Carmelites of her time inflicted on
themselves, never had she fabricated more or less terrifying
spiritual ordeals for herself, in which one attaches a great importance to oneself, viewing oneself as one cursed by God
and sent by Him into the outer darkness.'' Yet, just like that,
out of the blue, she experiences the trial of the night. And to
an extreme degree: ''You really believe, do you, that the mist
which hangs about you will clear away later on? All right, all
right, go on longing for death! But death will make nonsense
of your hopes: it will only mean a night darker than ever, the
night of mere non-existence.''² We cannot help but notice the
last two words, padded, felted, which point to a death,
period. Forevermore. It is not even the death from which we
could draw overtones of romanticism, color and lyric poems,
it is not the ''winding sheet of purple in which slumber the
dead gods,'' but total effacement in the fog, an entombment
in nothingness and meaninglessness. ''The night of mere non-
existence.'' And it is at this point that St. Thérèse says forthwith: ''But how can I go on writing about it without running
the risk of talking blasphemously? As it is I'm terrified of
having said too much.''³

It is necessary to dwell on her real state, such as she dares
to describe it, with a faithfulness that must need astonish us,
without a trace of exhibitionism. It is necessary to dwell on
the denseness of the darkness that surrounds her: she did not
let herself be taken in with fine words, not even her own. But
this ''darkness'' has a difference in relation to the ''night'' of
the Spanish Carmelite. John of the Cross lived at a time in
which to all intents and purposes almost everybody believed
in God. And his spiritual quest was lived in a kind of face to
face with God before whom the human being views himself as
infinitely poor, infinitely nothing, nothingness. Thérèse of
Lisieux's experience takes place in a time in which atheism

begins to install itself on a massive scale: a time in which Charles de Foucauld was to be an unbeliever for twelve years, between 1874 and 1886, and primarily for philosophic reasons, a time in which Nietzsche wrote the conclusion of *Zarathustra,* in 1885. And in France people were beginning to become aware of this increasingly widespread atheism.

Yet Thérèse's experiences, which began on Eastertide of 1896, are indissolubly linked to the burgeoning awareness of this fact of atheism. From the very start of her account, and in order to make it understood, Thérèse describes the before and after of the ordeal of Easter of 1896. *Before:* "I couldn't believe that there really were godless people who had no faith at all: it was only by being false to his own inner convictions that a man could deny the existence of heaven." *After:* "But there are souls which haven't got any faith, which lose through misuse of grace, this precious treasure, fountain of all pure and true happiness. And, now in those happy days of Eastertide, Jesus taught me to realize that.'"[4] Before she had thought that atheism was a flaunted position, a sham. After, she perceived that unbelievers really exist. And she considers—and this is fundamental—that this new view that she has of unbelievers is due to Jesus himself, that it is a grace to have had her eyes opened and to finally have seen that unbelievers exist. And it is immediately after this awareness, and through it, that Thérèse is invaded "by an impenetrable darkness."

Thus here we are no longer before a night of faith in which the human being, in a lone face-to-face with God, loses his foothold and discovers himself as nothingness. Rather, we are before a state in which the unbelief of Thérèse's contemporaries, at a single blow, interrogates this young Carmelite to the depths of her being. It is an interrogation, but not a destruction, of her faith. It is an ambivalent state in which Thérèse participates in the darkness—the "darkness" "that could not recognize him for what he was, the King of

Light!'', and in which, at the same time, she participates in
this light given by Jesus. "But here I am Lord . . . to whom
your divine light has made itself known."[5] The two sentences
follow each other and neither the one nor the other can be
suppressed.

Accordingly Thérèse's mystical state was to be that of finding herself in a situation that, at first sight, was absurdly contradictory. She does not cease to participate in the light of the
faith and at the same time she participates in the darkness in
which unbelievers live. She is immersed in suffering never experienced previously and in a joy greater than she ever felt
before: "And so, though it robs me of all enjoyment of life,
this ordeal God has sent me, I can still tell him that everything
he does is delightful to me" (Ps. 92). But we must look closely into the reasons for this joy: she thinks that if Jesus has
made her see the reality of unbelief and has made her participate in the night of unbelief, it is only so that she may turn
the tables: so that she may live this state of darkness for the
sake of unbelievers themselves. And, consequently, for her it
is a new joy that she had never experienced until then—and
for a very good reason!—the joy of not living the joy of faith
so that precisely these "others," these unbelievers who do
not know this joy, might finally attain to it: "What does it
matter, that I should catch no glimpse of its (heaven)
beauties, here on earth, if that will help poor sinners to see
them in heaven."[6]
Thus it was not a very lofty conceptual interrogation on
God that led Thérèse to this night as a sharing of life with
Jesus and unbelievers at one at the same time. It is, in fact,
astonishing to note that Thérèse becomes the "companion"
of unbelievers. "Companion," "pal," that is to say those
who share the same bread. She wants to eat at their table.
From the moment that she knows of the existence of
unbelievers, Thérèse does not view them condescendingly like

most of the religious of her time who became victims for sinners and thus became mothers to them bearing them, as it were, the life of faith. Thérèse regards them as her "brothers" and concerns herself only with being at the same "table" with them. "Lord, one of your own children, to whom your divine light has made itself known . . . by way of asking pardon for these brothers of mine, I am ready to live on a starvation diet as long as you will have it so."[7] Her concern is to remain with those who eat the bread of unbelief: she does not want to "rise from this unappetizing meal." She is prepared, she says, to remain there as the last one until "all those who have no torch of faith to guide them catch sight, at least, of its rays." "Let me go on there alone, taking my fill of trials, until you are ready to receive me into your bright kingdom."[8]

This manner of sharing the bread of unbelief is at the same time a manner of breaking bread with Jesus, of sharing the eucharistic table: for it is Jesus who has led her to this table of unbelievers. Of this she is certain. It is there, at this table, that she has taken a further step in the faith and in hope. Speaking of this ordeal, she says in June 1897: " . . . now it only serves to purge away all that natural satisfaction which my longing for heaven might have brought me."[9] And it is also there, at this table of unbelievers that she knows perfect joy. We recall here that in the *Little Flowers* of St. Francis of Assisi, he knows perfect joy when upon arriving, in the snow and wind, before the monastery, he is not recognized by the porter and thus cast outside by his brothers. For Thérèse, the perfect joy is to find herself among unbelievers and, eating at their table, to be shaken by their questions while remaining in the faith. She compares herself to a storm-tossed "chick not yet fledged": "I find it difficult to believe in the existence of anything except the clouds which limit my horizon. It's only then that I realize the possibilities of my weakness; find consolation in staying at my post, and directing my gaze towards one invisible light which communicates itself, now, only in the eye of faith.''[10]

This consolation is also an extraordinary joy that she experiences. She compares what she is about to experiment with—hope in the night at the heart of the encounter with the unbelievers, and the joys of the Beyond. And, speaking to Jesus himself, she doesn't hesitate to affirm: "And yet, I don't think I shall really regret having aspired to the highest levels of love, even if it doesn't mean attaining them hereafter: unless, after death, the memory of all my earthly hopes disappears by some miracle, that memory will always be my consolation.''[11]

Thus the more a human being advances in the Christian faith, the more he lives the presence of God as an absence, the more he accepts to die to the idea of becoming aware of God, of fathoming him. For he has learned, while advancing, that God is unfathomable. And thenceforth the presence of God assumes value in his eyes only against a backdrop of absence. The mystic, in his long and complicated pilgrimage, experiences an alternation of the presence and of the absence of God. But, by degrees, the absence of God is felt more and more and the mystic understands that the absence is primary, essential. Never will he possess God, never will he totally encircle him. God, like a great love in the life of a human, will always remain "other," that is, always in some way "mystery." The mystic does not think that Jesus is the agency through which he will recuperate God: he affirms that the notion of grasping God must be renounced, that one must die to all this all-too-human will to appropriate God. The mystic wants to burn away this nostalgia that dwells in the heart of man and which consists in the effort to re-find God as an object of childhood, one irremediably lost. At the beginning of the mystical life, of the really Christian life, there is the acquiescence in a fundamental lack. In the same way as it is explained in the beginning of Genesis: man is not God and will never be able to be him. The Christian mystic admits that he is not a particle of God and that he will not dissolve in God. And he announces that this acquiescence not to be God is tantamount, most particularly, to "paradise," and already on earth. For the one who wishes himself God or who takes himself for God, or still, the one who deems that he possesses God because he believes in Him are persons affected by a dangerous paranoia. And they oppress others with a power that they define as divine in consequence of which they crush man under their all-powerful laws, their inquisitions, their gulags, their concentration camps. On the contrary, the true mystic is a being of peace who does not want to possess others nor the world, just as he does not want to possess God. John XXIII demonstrated this before our very own eyes.

Thus the mystic is someone who has had a long term confrontation with God, like Jacob in the struggle that he waged all through the night, someone who does not cease to confront God—because the temptation to possess God is inherent in man. Rather, he is someone who, at the same time—and that is the act of faith at its peak—accepts the notion that God has existed and exists before him and that God has loved him and loves him before him. God always precedes us, we see Him only from behind, he walks ahead, he is ahead of us.

The Night of Jesus

What the mystic experiences—and every Christian is a mystic because it is not the great illuminations that are the mark of the mystic but the night, an everyday night—is a kind of distancing from God in proportion to advances in the deepening of his faith. Jesus also lives this experience, and it is very important to see this.

The manner in which one spoke of Jesus, up until very recently, was strongly stamped by what in theological jargon is called "monophysism": an insistence on the divinity of Christ to such a degree that Christ's very humanity is absorbed by it, so that we are presented with a bloodless Jesus, stripped of his human flesh, emptied even of his human consciousness. Less than twenty years ago, a professor of theology of recognized competence, affirmed before his students that in the boat in the center of the storm on the Sea of Tiberias, although Jesus was asleep, actually, thanks to his divinity, he saw everything that was happening and waited until the storm—as well as the ordeal of the apostles—was at its height before intervening and saving them from danger. This Jesus who sleeps only with one eye, or still, whose right eye has a divine gaze whereas his left eye has a human gaze is, of course, even worse than the one proposed in the milieu of Saint-Sulpice. It will be noted that he is sadistic, that he extends his aid only after letting them stew in anxiety and fear. This twofold gaze renders him inhuman. Jesus did not play that game, a perverse game which men often like to play, a game in which they have decked out Jesus as a participant.

In the gospels we see a Jesus altogether different from this portrait of a being at once god, demi-god, superman and perverse master. Jesus, throughout his life, experiences tormenting conflicts in his relations with God, and not the problem-free harmony that has been assuringly handed down to us. Many Christians reject this image of a torn Jesus, hesitant in the mission that God has entrusted to him. Let them therefore re-read the gospels and linger awhile over the symmetrical accounts that are found at the dawn and in the twilight of Jesus' public life: the temptation in the Desert, the agony in the Garden. In the desert, the place where man is confronted with the great choices of his life, Jesus undergoes an intense self-questioning on the means to take in order to carry out his mission. He is tempted to resort to certain means but upon looking at them full in the face, he discerns that they are not means according to God: to give men material nourishment only, to provoke fate and God himself, to kneel down before the world are ways that are not those of God. And Jesus, after an inner struggle—and there was an inner struggle—rejects all these forms of power, of magic and of demagogy.

The same self-questioning was to reproduce itself in Jesus' consciousness throughout his public life, and the course that he followed was to be a constant demarcation in the face of these diabolical methods where it would be a question of taking possession of men in the name of God. That is not what Jesus wants. And when we see him dominate the dark forces that ravage human beings, it is because he himself has dominated the temptations in himself. And he knows that these temptations ever return in force: he who has cleansed his consciousness in the desert and purged his heart of the lusts for power, knows that they are ever ready to re-implant themselves: "When an unclean spirit goes out of a man it wanders through waterless country looking for a place to rest, and cannot find one. 'Then it says, I will return to the home I come from' " (Mt. 12, 43-44). And we know that finding this home "unoccupied, swept and tidied" it will immediately set out in search of other sirens who, along with it, will begin to sing their seductive songs.

Jesus therefore was to wage this struggle against sirens and seducers all through his life. He was even to be on guard against his friends, such as Peter, who understand nothing and who do not hesitate to sin against the Spirit, to lead him into the temptation of power.

If only God would speak in a clear manner! If only God would intervene in his favor and lead him to success! But in the very measure that Jesus advances, in the same measure does he experience uncertainties and anxieties. He declares

himself "troubled" in the bottommost depth of his being.
And in the last days of his life, he descends the staircase of
solitude, step by step. God seems to abandon him to his fate.
The failures are there, patent, and they are the signs, above
all in the religious milieu of his time, of a refusal by God to
accord him accreditation. And, without let-up, Jesus must go
forth to the encounter with his Israelite roots and his Juda-
eity: he must re-ascend the religious current, terrible and
strong as a mountain stream, according to which God
rewards the good and punishes the wicked, according to
which if someone is blind, he has well-deserved this
darkness—he has sinned, either in person or through his
parents. And in all his being, Jesus was deeply affected when
the high priests, the doctors of the Law, but also the passers-
by even at the foot of his cross, came to tempt him for the
purpose of making him lose hope: "He puts his trust in God;
now let God rescue him if he wants him."

Jesus experienced the extreme of dereliction. When, pro-
nouncing on the cross the first words of the psalm, "My God,
my God, why have you deserted me?", Jesus wants to express
the meaning of the whole of the psalm, he wants to cry out to
the people from which he stems that human failure and even
spiritual failure is not the sign of rejection on the part of God
and he reveals that even in failure one can continue to trust in
God and continue to declare: "Then I shall proclaim your
name to my brothers," as in fact the psalm states.

But how can we fail to see that this psalmody of Jesus on
the cross is the expression, once more, of a temptation overcome, of a despair outrun? Faith, trust, hope are not natural
to man. Religion, law, sentence, indeed are natural to man
and he does not deprive himself of them. But to reveal, in the
very heart of failure and at the hour of death, amid human
clamor and the silence of God, that God is Love, is that not
precisely the true, intense and free acknowledgment of God?
And is it not a turning of one's back, in a manner more vic-

torious than any other, on the temptation of unbelief? Evil, wretchedness, failure are, in effect, the first grounds of unbelief and this is understandable: how can one not curse God and despair when evil is there period, and heaven seems emtpy? Jesus overcame this temptation.

The cry that Jesus uttered on the cross— "a loud voice," says Scripture, must not be romanticised but, rather, taken in its precise texture. The habitual cry of man before death is a cry of rejection, of anxiety and even of terror. Jesus had lived this very cry, in agony, in the Garden of Olives—the word agony, moreover, means struggle. His agony had been a struggle against the shadow, against death, with life that formulates the question: "Why death, why must it come to that?" Death is then present to him as a "cup" that must be drained. The four evangelists take up this word again which in the Old Testament is applied to those who are unfaithful to God. God reserves for them this "cup of reeling," "the wine of rage" which makes them disappear from his face. Jesus, thus, drains the "cup" which is normally allotted only to unbelievers. This term also means the ordeal undergone by the just. Thérèse of Lisieux did likewise when she was to express the wish to seat herself "at the table of sinners."

In the agony, he drinks from this "cup" which is bitter, he will drain it to the dregs. The point at issue is the totality of unbeliefs of men in the face of evil and death who say, "God cannot exist, Love does not exist." Upon recalling that she was affected with tuberculosis and doomed to an early death, Thérèse of Lisieux was to live an agony of the same kind, for eighteen months. She knew the night of faith. She was tempted to hurl herself into death, "a night darker than ever, the night of mere non-existence." She, too, drank from this cup, the cup of man's despair in relation to God without, however, by so doing losing trust. Jesus, in the agony, assumes the global incredulity of humanity. He does so from within his own trust, in the historical and religious situation of his time. And it must be clearly seen that in order to do so and thus assume it, he had to surmount the religious aberrations of the pharisees—aberrations that permitted someone to believe himself justified through his own merits. Thérèse of Lisieux was to do likewise when she differentiated herself from her sisters, the religious of the Carmel of Lisieux, who gave themselves to God as "victims" for sinners, and who had as a base the same pharasaical attitude of seeing themselves above sinners. And in the same way as Jesus, Thérèse rejected "merits": she wanted to arrive "empty-handed" before God. This form of unbelief which consists in basing oneself on one's belief in order to believe oneself superior to others is a particularly offensive form that has estranged so many from the Christian faith—for pharisees have the gift of presenting their practices as being the sole and unique authentic expression of faith. "Pious as angels, proud as devils," said Sainte-Beuve of the religious of Port-Royal. And closer to us, Léon Bloy who had been much criticized in his village by very pious persons who never failed to go to church to revere the eucharistic presence, said of them: "They adore themselves before the Holy Sacrament." Throughout the gospels we see that Christ was nauseated in the presence of this warmed over religious, unbelieving, pharisaical stench, spotless like whitewashed tombs that look lovely on the outside but which stink horribly within. He denounces these unbelieving pharisees who clean "the outside of the cup" but who inside themselves "are filled with extortion and wickedness" (Lk. 11, 39), who "load on men burdens that are unendurable" which they make not the slightest effort to relieve. Jesus asks that one fear these so religious men because they do not only have the power to kill one but to make one lose hope and to plunge into unbelief (Lk. 12, 5). So often has a person's religious comportment and Christian faith been confused, that we are hardly mistrustful of all those who outwardly manifest a spectacular religious attitude while forgetting that their leaven ("the leaven of the pharisees," said Jesus) has the capacity to spoil the whole dough, to render the bread inedible. A history of unbelief is yet to be written—beginning with the bad fruits that it produces, beginning with the scandals that it provokes in the hearts of children.

We can be sure that Jesus had that leaven, those fruits on his heart more particularly than all the others, more strongly than pagan or indifferent belief. It is very easy to embrace a great cause, to die for a beloved homeland, but to find oneself face to face with perverse individuals of hypocritically sanctimonious mien and of impure heart, to witness the works of death to which they give birth and to take their acts upon oneself without striking at them and rejecting them but, instead, performing one's own acts that transcend theirs and opening a path through all this rottenness, that certainly must not have been an alluring prospect. This cup was particularly bitter and we can understand why Christ uttered that cry of disgust in the Garden.

It was a cry of a different kind of Golgotha. A dying man rattles and groans. He expires while losing his breath, but he does not cry out because he wants to retain his breath to the very last. This cry, through its freedom, resembles the cry uttered by the infant at the moment of birth: and Jesus on the cross, far from despairing of his Father and no longer believing in him, sends him this cry which is the hope of a second birth, a radical surrender rooted in trust. It is not a cry for help, to be protected from evil-doers, it is not a cry for help like that of a child to his mother. It is not a cry for the purpose of preserving his dislocated body, of having it restored to its wholeness. It is an "amen," a "yes," just as the newborn infant says "yes" to life. Jesus says "yes" to life, to his Father, and that is why John the evangelist was able to say of Jesus that he is life: Jesus did not cease to believe in life.

Night According to John the Evangelist

It is quite striking upon frequent encounters with free-masons to note that even the most agnostic, or the most atheistic, among them gladly cites the Gospel of St. John and particularly the passages that refer to light: to be sure it is no more than a cultural reference to a symbolism that stirs them.

But if we take a closer look at the Johannine Gospel, in an altogether objective manner, we note that he speaks very much about light. And it is a light, in fact, that is tragically marked by "darkness." In her book *Approches de l'Évangile,*[12] Annie Jaubert rightly asserts: "The questions that the shock of incredulity posed to the evangelist and the answers that he gives make of him the theologian of non-faith as well as of faith. By virtue of this he is infinitely modern."

In the Johannine gospel there is a ceaseless presence of in-dividuals—Jews, pharisees, heads of the Temple, their identi-ty matters little—who are "unbelievers" in a fundamental sense. Jesus runs constantly into a wall of "non-believing." What he does, what he says meets with confusion, hostility and provokes division among his interlocutors. If some are inclined to believe, many others say of him that "he is raving," that "he is possessed" (10, 19-21), that he is a vile seducer (7, 12) and that, therefore, it is scandalous for anyone to place his trust in him.

John the evangelist is witness to this dramatic misunderstanding: Jesus' hearers have their ears sealed in the presence of what he said. He notes this incapacity of his hearers: "They did not believe in him . . . indeed, they were unable to believe" (12, 37-39). It is a misunderstanding which, moreover, is leading towards hate and persecution: "The hour is coming when anyone who kills you will think he is doing a holy duty for God," said Jesus to his apostles at the last Supper (16, 4-5).

Hence John notes the fact of "non-believing" and its immense force. And the power of "non-believing"—or of "darkness"—is so great that it constitutes an obstacle to light. From the outset non-acceptance is primary: "his own people did not accept him" (1, 11); the "darkness" is primary: the human condition is, primordially, to be in darkness. One passes from darkness to light, from death to life. Like the man born blind whose story John tells in his Gospel: he is blind, he was born thus. He is not guilty, moreover, just as we are not guilty of our native condition of opaqueness: it is a simple factual datum.

We see this man born blind progressively opens himself to the light which, little by little, unveils itself to him. He sees ever more clearly, whereas the pharisees sink ever more deeply in the fog. Those who believe they see become blind, while the man born blind acquires the eyes of faith. God has acted within the very darkness and has invited us to a walk towards the light.

But in order to be liberated by God and opened to his light, like the man born blind, one must extricate oneself from the walls in which one is self-imprisoned. John admirably describes the state of mind of the pharisees and of the Jews in general: they are people who enjoy privileges, they are behind their impenetrable walls with their convictions and their "orthodoxy," they are like enlightened beings who glory in their state and are perfectly closed in on themselves. There is no crack, no interstice through which the light of faith could make a breach: "How can you believe, since you look to one another for approval," Jesus points out to them. It is a self-sufficiency against which nobody can do anything. And this self-sufficiency rots all the actions of those who live according to it: for they exist and they act only in order to reinforce their own "ego." How could they hearken to Jesus and recognize him, if they are permeable only to their own convictions?

How pierce the wall of "non-believing?" John was to

answer, symbolically, in speaking of living water or of breath: he affirms therewith his hope in God who is capable of piercing through this wall of unbelief. The Spirit comes in effect and assumes Jesus' defense, upsets his adversaries, reaches hearts: he shows them that Jesus' views were just, that he is truly the light and he unveils the meaning of the events that have unfolded: the life of Jesus, his death, his resurrection.

What is to be particularly retained from a reading of John the Evangelist is his insistence on what he has intensely observed: that belief is not natural to man. There is a "difficulty," congenital to man, in the matter of accepting God's testimony."[13]

In his Gospel John employs the expression "the sin of the world" (1, 30) only once: it is John the Baptist who declares that Jesus comes "to take away" this "sin of the world." What must be understood by that?

We have seen that the great mystics are marked by the night, by the feeling of the precariousness of their faith, by the conviction that the struggle of faith was to be resumed without let-up against the invasion of the darkness of non-believing, that incredulity was constantly being re-born, that God alone finally could have the last word in the face of the darkness and in the "night of non-existence," as Thérèse of Lisieux put it. And for these men of faith that mystics are by definition, Christ is the only one to have victoriously affronted the radical ordeal of trust in God.

For unbelievers Jesus' failure led to his execution by the religious leaders of his time and shows clearly that God did not render himself evident to man. Otherwise, on the grounds of inner logic, all Jesus' hearers should have had to believe in God. It happens that one meets unbelievers who regret their unbelief and who have a "bad" and guilty conscience. Now what John the evangelist shows clearly is that non-believing is primary, that man does not immediately acquiesce in trust in

God: that such a trust requires a slow journey, and that God in no case short-circuits the road to human freedom.

The Night of Non-Believing

In Jesus, through the radical "yes" that he expresses to God, man escapes from the closed circle, from the fatality of unbelief. Through Jesus, faith irrupts in the world and, thenceforth, death which is non-believing is definitively overcome. Life is here—the gospel calls the Risen Christ "The Living One." The Risen Christ is the mediator, the ferryman who, in a decisive manner, has brought man out of his condition in which he was going around in circles, namely from that condition marked by the impossibility of perceiving any horizon other than that of non-believing. Thenceforth faith is possible, it is "already there," it is an opening and a liberation.

Jesus, in his final and decisive "yes" snaps the universal struggle between faith and unbelief that all men have ceaselessly lived in their being. He gives peace to men, reconciling them with themselves first of all, breaking the alienation in which they find themselves, namely the impossibility of envisaging a way out of their non-believing. Any person of good will can recognize that Jesus never ceased to trust in God even up to the very moment of his death. And perhaps, recognizing this fact, such a person will take another step forward upon pondering the fact that God responded to this trust of Jesus by a "new birth," the resurrection. But, at least, such a person will be liberated from the dark horizon that is the radical impossibility of putting his trust in another, upon seeing that Jesus, freely, in his life and death, was someone who had trusted the Other, who had presented himself to the Other, and had abandoned himself to him, by being true and disarmed. And to believe in the Risen Christ is to believe that to this "yes" of Jesus, God had responded by a new "yes" to men, the "yes" of God to man being the one in which he had caused man and his freedom to spring up. To believe in the Risen Christ is to believe that through this "yes" of Jesus, God breaks through and gives birth to a new humanity. Up to the moment of this "yes" men were primarily locked in incredulity. Jesus comes to break this circle and this propensity of man to "non-believing." He opens hearts to trust in God who then responded and who does not cease to respond now to man through the Risen Christ.

It is necessary to reflect deeply on this propensity to non-believing which indwells in man and whose force John clearly reveals. It is a propensity that we can call "the sin of the world," while being careful to remove from the word "sin" the overly individualist connotation that is usually given to it, namely a puerile manner of mediocre transgression of the Law, on the sly, and thereafter to have a morbid sense of culpability in regard to it that imprisons us in an egocentric and prolonged delectation.. Yet, it is precisely this very conception that causes one to participate in "sin of the world" and to reinforce it. True sin always masks itself. The "sin of the world" is lived by a man when he deludes himself about himself, about others and about God. To "hoax" oneself, to delude oneself, to become the prince of one's own illusion, such is the mask worn by "the sin of the world." The one who acquiesces in faith passes through a baptism, through the water that is first and foremost a death, the death of the illusions and delusions with which one saddles oneself. When Christ asks that one "leave his father and mother" it is not primarily a matter of leaving the family dwelling as such but, rather, a matter of breaking with the deluding images of a paradise of childhood, it is a matter of accepting the fact that Eden is irretrievably lost and that life must go on against a backdrop of loss and not against a backdrop of possession. The one who does not accept this loss and who clings to a possession, to a past, to a treasure—familial, social, religious—prevents himself or herself from advancing. He or she remains alienated and unfulfilled.

And it goes without saying, as we see among the Jews through the Johannine gospel, it is precisely in the religious domain that one can delude oneself in the most subtle and most irremediable manner. What did the Jews demand? Extraordinary signs on the part of God. They wanted dazzling miracles, triumphal attestations of God. For which Jesus sharply reproached them. And when Jesus expels the thieves from the Temple, we must see in this happening much more than an expression of holy rage: the fact is that Jesus cannot endure those who "steal," those who, like the pharisees, present themselves as the possessors of God, those who confiscate God. Believers are exposed to this supreme unbelief which is then sin against the Spirit. If the pharisees are so furious against Jesus, it is because he has unveiled before their very own eyes—they were not conscious of their own deceit vis-a-vis themselves—their "self-hoaxing." They thought that they were truly adoring and serving God and here is Jesus who points out to them that they are doing naught else but seeking themselves. How could they endure this lucidity that scalds them? But, thenceforth, the dice are cast. From the moment Jesus has shown the light, they must choose: to remain in their "possessiveness" of God or to undergo a change of heart and vision. Which Jesus clearly perceives: "If I had not performed such works among them as no one else has ever done, they would be blameless; but as it is, they have seen all this" (15, 24). Jesus thus acts as a "revealer" of this deep-rooted sin. Jesus is like a sword of fire that leads consciences to decide, a sword that effects the separation between light and darkness. Jesus shows the pharisees—and all men—that they give themselves a good "conscience" by self-justifying themselves and thus considering themselves as gods, sure of themselves, of their good right, of their "orthodoxy." Jesus, through his word, his silences and his deeds leads constantly to a "judgment," a true analysis, a clear discernment: "and indeed everybody who does wrong hates the light and avoids it for fear his actions should be exposed." He exposes the interior illusions and delusions. Any attentive reader of the gospel cannot help but meet this look of Jesus that discriminates, that burns all that which is but sham and leads each one "to usher in truth." Before this look of Jesus some flee—among them believers themselves—and among them who call themselves, or who are called, unbelievers. Belief and unbelief are not in a formula, but in the heart.

Non-Believing and Christians

The sin against the Spirit, such is the foundation of non-believing, according to St. John. It consists much more in the act of wanting to take possession of God than in the act of rejecting God and of declaring oneself an atheist. For with the one who declares himself an atheist or an agnostic there can be an honesty in his recognition that, for man, God is "an ocean for which we have neither bark nor sail" as Littré said. The atheist is frequently a person who finds the conviction that one possesses *The Truth* outrageous, pretentious, if not delirious, that one knows what it's all about on the subject of God. In that category we find many Christians who are first and foremost deists: for them God appears evident and that he exists is taken for granted. For them, belief is natural to man. Consequently these Christians affirm, and often in order to reassure themselves, that man is naturally believing and that he turns immediately, through a kind of spontaneous movement of his being, towards "the one who has made the heaven and the earth." But what does this movement toward a beyondness of self, a beyondness of the planet, a beyondness of history signify? Is it not simply an "oceanic movement," the recognition of coming from a great Whole and the aspiration to return to it, the nostalgia for the maternal womb, which was liquid, calm and warm? Many who have simply remained faithful to the primal matrix and consider themselves linked to it think of themselves as believers: consequently with all their might they want to find this primordial environment, plunge into it anew, and no longer have to undergo the experience of painful ruptures and the incessant march of everyday life and of the existence of men in time and society. One could give a thousand examples of this pantheist and puerile attitude.

Unbelief is man's normal tendency. Christian faith is difficult. It is still a form of unbelief, and this should be easy to understand, to remain attached to the nostalgia of a lost childhood and to try to find it again by decking out this need in Christian colors. Christ himself, moreover, is often apprehended as the one who will permit the conquest of this new maternal womb. Christ is reduced to the rank of an instrument, a gadget: many Christians utilize him as a means for achieving their ends, that is, as the means to recover God to their own advantage.

The same process is found in relation to the Church. The Jews, in the time of Jesus, demanded convincing miracles by God, signs that would demonstrate God's existence and his omnipotence. The Jews demanded from Jesus a Kingdom that is of this world and that would make them kings of the world. They wanted him to be a Messiah with whom they could identify and who would make their race the first in the universe. For this very reason the Jews were scandalized by Christ's weakness and by the crucified condition of Jesus and they were scandalized by the God whom he had proclaimed: a God of weakness, of vulnerability, of humility. The mortal humanity of the Son of God become man, such was the stumbling-block for the whole of the Jews, including the apostles. They wanted a strong God, for what would be the use of confiscating a weak God? And what a derision to appropriate to oneself a Kingdom that is made of poverty, of gentleness, of the inverse of riches and of power? If the Jews wanted no part of the God that Jesus taught them, it was because this God ran counter to the desire of possession and because he invited them no longer to appropriate either others or God himself to themselves.

Christians on the whole—save for some integralists—no longer demand dazzling and absolutely convincing manifestations of the Omnipotence of God. They no longer pray that the fire of heaven descend to exterminate unbelievers. But, nevertheless, their request remains identical, it has merely shifted to the Church. Many Christians have made the Church the equal of God, whereas she is the bride of Christ and his sacrament. Many have made of her the Mother Supreme whereas she is the servant of God like Mary of Nazareth. Consequently they would like the Church to show her strength to men, to be the unbreakable rock of humanity. They forget that the Church is a storm-tossed bark and that she must keep afloat in the midst of storms and not want smugly to gain a port of haven without difficulty. They would like the Church to be like an absolutely pure and attractive bride who seduces all of humankind and lets it enter into the fold of faith and Christianity on a massive scale. This is the image of a Church that is the object of a dream, a Church that is imagined as an "omnipotence." This is a comportment that can only be described as childish. For then Christians resemble children who see their father and their mother as prodigious giants, they have a nostalgia for the time in which they saw their parents as faultless beings. These Christians want to reconstruct this lost time and construct, in compensation for the parental failure, a Church that is equal to their dreams. In order to advance, in order to become an adult, every human being must renounce these imaginary, ideal and immortal parents. Likewise must most Christians renounce this imaginary Church and accede to the humble truth of God, of Christ and of the Church. Christians find it difficult to accept the idea that the Church is at once "saint and sinner" as Yves Congar says. And they have likewise insisted on the divinity of Christ in order to blur what scandalized them as a sign of weakness: the humanity of Christ. Just as, likewise, they have a tendency to mask the poverties of the Church and to make of her a superpower, moral or spiritual to be sure, but nevertheless a superpower if not more. All too often, the Church, for the Christian, assumes the contours of mythic parents, even more grandiose than them, because she is marked by a divine sign. The process by which citizens are manipulated by a dictator or by a totalitarian State have been analyzed for a long time and in depth: they are exalted by making them adhere to a kind of giant with whom they identify through paranoic projections. There is a precise unbelief that lies in wait for Christians: to make of the Church a spiritual ensemble equal to God himself, to make of her an idol from whom they can again get something, that is to say, their self-sufficiency. These Christians are offended when it is pointed out to them that they are imprisoning themselves in an oedipal relation with the Mother Supreme, in whom they find a narcissistic certitude and a monolithic assurance. It constitutes, however, a subtle and very resistant form of "non-believing" into which beings who deem themselves Christians sometimes lapse. At times unbelief lurks where we do not believe it to be.

THE ARDENT ABSENCE OF GOD

Christian faith exists—this was the subject of the whole preceding chapter—not on the basis of an evident and indisputable presence but, rather, on the acceptance of a non-possession of God against a backdrop of absence. The mystic—any Christian—is the one who participates in "the intimacy of his ardent Absence" (R. M. Rilke). When Jesus reveals to us the God who is, he unveils to us primarily that God cannot be a graspable object but that he is "beyondness." At the same time, however, he points out to us that we can approach him more and more each day of our lives. How? Through Christ, the humanity of the Risen Christ. This is the essential message of the four gospels which, each in its own manner, present this New Man who speaks to us of God and who can lead us to Him if we so wish.

Accordingly the Christian faith involves, before all else, a break—a break with all the possible ways with which we imagine we can possess God. The Christian is the one who, first of all, is intimately convinced that he or she will never possess God, not even in Heaven, above all in Heaven—for Heaven primarily is the resolve no longer to want to be or to "have" God. And thus to be in peace.

An Appropriated God

Consequently, the first unbelief is not primarily that of men and women who, since the 18th century were bent upon affirming that God does not exist. Rather, it is the unbelief of those, of all times and everywhere, but especially in Christianity and among Christians who, acting in a more or less disguised but positive way that nevertheless reveals the secret of their hearts, would try to lay hold of God. Thus many believe in God in order to appropriate him. Here, strictly speaking, it is a matter of an unbelief, of a most deeply rooted unbelief. If a man tells a woman that he loves her, but only for the purpose of appropriating her, we understand that this man has even less love for her in his heart than a man who is indifferent to this woman, or than another who honestly tells her that he doesn't love her. For in the honest declaration there can still be an esteem for the other, and there is a neutrality in the indifference. But in the will to possession that assumes the features of love, there is a matter of a wolf in sheep's clothing, it is a matter of perversity, of a utilization of love for an end that is alien to it.

It will be objected that many believers sincerely believe that they love God, and that they do not look only for their self-interest, a personal reward, an enlargement of their ego etc. This sincerity is not being questioned here: many Christians are unconscious of their real reasons for belief, they delude themselves. Jesus on the cross could say: "Father forgive them; they do not know what they are doing." And the Father forgives, of course, such a lack of awareness and such an inconsistency. The Father is not deaf to this call of his son and to his understanding of the human being who constantly tries to be God. And when one notes this deep-rooted unbelief of Christians themselves, it is not because one places oneself on a plane with the chief star Sirius, or because one takes the place of God in order to judge from on high. For every Christian knows that he is an unbeliever who is ignorant of the depth of his unbelief. And the Christian is precisely the one who, quietly, asks Christ's help: "Lord, I believe; help my unbelief!" For the Christian clearly knows that in the depth of his heart, as in that of every human being, there dwells unbelief. The only difference between the Christian and the one with convictions other than those of the

Christian faith, is that the former has trust in Christ who alone can deliver him from unbelief, he has trust in Christ who has already delivered, potentially, all men from nonbelieving and who never ceases to aid human beings to pass on to the act of belief, to lean on him in order constantly to overcome the assaults of unbelief and to live in the faith.

What we are witnessing in our days—and this is called the crisis of Christianity—is primarily a crisis over the nature of God in the Christian communities. A number of them have become aware of their unawareness: they have begun to take account of the indecency and of the enormity, of the fatuousness and of the senseless error contained in the pretention to "possess" God. In consequence of this, they have tried to find out the meaning of the Church.

The God who has all too often been presented by the Churches, as a matter of fact, has been a simple product of deists. He is a being who organizes the universe and the existence of humankind through a certain number of imperatives.

God is presented as a keystone. A virtuous atheist is utterly inconceivable. According to the affirmations of Vatican Council I, held one hundred years ago, one who is an atheist can become such only for two reasons: either because he is secretly immoral or because he lacks intelligence. These affirmations were shared by all the deists of the same time and by those among them who were the most resolute enemies of the Catholic Church: in their view, the existence of God is the sole rock on which order and morality can be based, and they pointed out that the greatest number of criminals were found among atheists.

God was thus a principle that orders the course of the universe, who has programmed the history of the world and of humanity and he makes this history advance towards its consummation. All is subjected—being and becoming—to his laws and to his decrees. He has established a natural order, a natural law to which one must perforce submit if one wants to achieve success in life and be assured of some future. Outside his power, there is no salvation.

The Churches have closely copied this model of God. Like this God, they have established themselves as the sole sources of knowledge and power, defining themselves as the sole holders of the forces of God. They have effected a structuralization of the whole of social life and of the whole of everyday existence. They hold the supreme keys, the decisive judgment on all being and on all things. Those who deviated, those who were heretics were "lost" and they were "ostracized." Outside the Church, there is no salvation.

The societies that were constituted parallel to this image of God and that transmitted this image of God to humanity, consequently, set up keystones: popes or kings, czars or princes, in short, personages who represented the supreme keystone. At a lower degree, priests and clerics were ordained to recall to the people the norms and values and to deduce from them the meaning of everyday happenings as well as the great events of world history. Thus, around this keystone, we find concentric circles that were more or less close to the central point: the nobles, then the men of arms, then the men of law and, finally, the laborers in the field and on the lowest step, the foreigners. Each one was in his place and by virtue of this fact cohesiveness was always constantly and flawlessly maintained since it was a matter of gravitating around the central axis with the greatest possible fidelity.

It would be wrong to assume that this schema is something outmoded in the mind of Christians as a body. The way in which papal infallibility has often been presented by theologians and, even more, as it has been perceived by the mass of Christians, participates in this concentric schema. And it is the same presentation that prevails in the encyclical of Paul VI *Ecclessiam suam:* at the center is the Roman Catholic Church, around her the other Christians, further from the center, there is another circle: the adepts of the non-Christian religions; and finally, a last circle, the outermost one: the unbelievers.

Presentations of this kind were bound to be perceived as signs of domination: there are those who are close to God and who even "possess" the truth and there are those who deviate from the center and who are in the "outer darkness": the good, the less good and finally the wicked.

All these representations derive from a conception in which one short-circuits the present universe, history and the social data in order to refer everything to an ideal world, to another world, to a "hinter-world." Supreme existence is ascribed to this other world and one believes, all things considered, that human life—especially the one led by unbelievers without reference to the "other life" is a negligible quantity. So great is the insistence that all the social space belongs to God and to this other life that not only does the reference to God become imperative but the reference to man is judged to be of minor importance and, at times, unimportant. God is thus perceived as that which gives an answer to everything, decisively and definitively. It is significant that for unbelievers, Christians are viewed as beings who have found an answer to the questions of man and who are anchored in an unbreakable certitude. In their view, the Christian faith condemns its followers to fix themselves in positions that escape the essential questioning—the very questioning that is characteristic of the human being. And they are very astonished when they are told that our faith puts us in an unstable position respecting God, and that it enjoins us to continually deepen and examine our positions, positions that we ceaselessly run the risk of rigidifying, whereas human beings ought to try always to understand the meaning of the adventure of life afresh.

A Subversive God

Here we encounter once more the question of the primary unbelief that manifests itself in man in his craving to possess God. To make God the keystone of the universe—material through creation, or moral through conscience—is to try to seize the keystone, to place oneself in a dominating position, above others and history: above all and everybody.

Two recent anecdotes illustrate the very great difficulty Christians have in the matter of relinquishing this keystone God where they all too easily derive benefits and advantages.

In a TV program on *Jesus* on Easter-tide of 1975, unbelievers were gathered together with a Protestant, two Catholic priests and a rabbi. The latter rightly declared that the term "Son of God" was frequently employed in Scriptures to indicate someone who was trying to live his faith as a good Israelite. And a Christian exegete, moreover, could have immediately added that Jesus had never clearly declared his identity as "Son of God" in the sense in which Christians too often understand it: a kind of superman, or demiurge, a being who above all is no longer truly a man in order to be really, fully God. It must also be recalled that in the course of history many beings have claimed to be God or the incarnation of God and it is not by such an affirmation that Jesus would necessarily furnish the certitude of his divine filiation. In this program I was the last to be questioned by the interviewer. He asked: "At bottom, how do you view Jesus?" I replied:

"A very strong personality, with an extraordinary tenderness, a true prophet, he has all the Life of God in him, and he is truly risen, risen even today." How could one say any more in a few words that Jesus is truly the Son of God except by saying—in order to be understood by our contemporaries—"He has all the Life of God in Him." But for some Christian integralists it would have been necessary merely to employ the words of the past, the formulation of the old catechism. And, for them, the first sentence which made mention of Christ's humanity and dwelt on his personality, was immediately perceived as reductive: to dwell on Christ's humanity seemed to diminish his divinity—truly an aberrant notion.

But, above all, there was the second part of the text and the great affirmation that Christ had not only risen yesterday, but that he exists today, living, in his condition of a resurrected being. Yet, on this score what a lag still obtains in the Christian people among whom the Resurrection has been for so long misunderstood!

Another recent event clearly illustrates this lag in faith in the dead and risen Christ. It transpired on the occasion of the translation of the liturgical texts in French. In 1970, integralist Christians were most particularly roused by a text read in the Mass on Palm Sunday: the christological hymn of the apostle Paul to the Phillipians aims to present Christ as a model of humility to Christians, and he underscores that unlike Adam, who wanted to make himself the equal of God, Christ took on the human condition, including death. Violent campaigns erupted in the integralist review which did not hesitate to accuse the bishops of heresy in connection with the first translation which, in their eyes, robbed Christ of his divinity:

> "Christ Jesus is the image of God
> but he willed not to conquer by force
> equality with God."

So the translator, with a greater precision stated:

> "Christ Jesus, while remaining the very image of God,
> had willed not to claim
> to be similar to God."

This sparked a new campaign. The episcopal Liturgical Commission then published in March 1971 an official communication. In reaction, an integralist review charged: "The bureaus know very well what they want to put into the skulls of the faithful: Jesus Christ is not God." We see to what lengths bad faith can go.

Catholics, for so long separated from the Bible, had lost the sense of Scripture. If they had had this sense they would have better grasped what the apostle Paul expressed: that Christ, in his Humanity, normally should have received as his due a superhuman power and light, but that he had renounced it and had taken on all the traits of a man among men. What this matter revealed, however, is that many Catholics cling to words, to the letter, that they think that a biblical text is susceptible of only a single translation and that this translation then would be a dogmatic definition. St. Thomas Aquinas always insisted that "words" and "things" are not to be confused. The terms that we employ never encompass the Real that is God, words are not magic formulas that permit one to lay hands on the mystery like proprietors who have the key to their houses. And it is on this magic sentiment that the integralists base themselves when without letup they lie in wait to seize upon the slightest changes of words or when they denounce the absence of a word.

Jesus, therefore, first of all did not claim to be God, he did not hoist himself on a pedestal while tiumphantly beating his chest in the manner of a Tarzan. He posed deeds, and deeds that compromised the God of Abraham, of Isaac and of Jacob. Deeds speak: "It is not those who say to me, 'Lord, Lord'." In the Gospel we are quite beyond proclamations: we are immersed in everyday life and in history. Jesus does not primarily teach a kind of new doctrine on God, he does not give an original definition of Yahweh. He gives God a precise role in human affairs, he involves him.

Let us recall the scene of Golgotha where Jesus' adversaries place before him this dilemma: you have delivered other men; now you can't save yourself. But if you come down from the cross, you would manifest that God acts with you and for you. These men, who thus drive Jesus "into a corner" are certain that he is an impostor. He had affirmed that he had a surety from God and had opposed them, the legitimate authorities who express the will of God. The death of Jesus, this crucified one whom God does not deliver, proves to them that they are in the right, that God is with them, and that they have acted with justice, according to God.

We find ourselves in the presence of two contrary conceptions of God: the God of the pharisees whom they believe they are recognizing by condemning to death this blasphemer named Jesus, and the God of Jesus whom Jesus is recognizing by not asking him to act efficaciously in order to save him from the crucifixion and by continuing to place his trust in him even at the moment of the ignominious death itself.

In his attitude, Jesus is faithful to the image of God that he has set forth throughout his existence. Not a God who strictly lays down principles that must be honored by general declarations. Rather, a God who always expresses himself at the level of the particular. It is easy to say that one adheres to a good God, full of tenderness and justice—this is what Jesus' adversaries said. But in a particular case, for example, this man whose right hand is withered (Lk. 6, 6-10) and who comes to Jesus to ask to be healed in a synagogue on the sabbath. Here the beautiful declarations are swept away, a decision must be taken, so Jesus asks the pharisees who are present: "Is it permissible to do good or to do evil on the sabbath, to save a life or to take it away?" They remain silent. They exalt the greatness and the honor of God as such and, accordingly, for them the sabbath is an absolute. For Jesus it is not the sabbath that is primary: "The sabbath was made for man." Jesus therefore does not refer to an absolute law, the honor of God does not dwell in the absolute and abstract perfection

of the Law or of the Temple. The disciple of the God of Jesus
is not the one who refers to a System, to a pre-established
casuistry. Jesus rejects the pharisees who know what each one
must do, who have God's plan and his volitions in their head,
who from on high issue orders and ukases in the name of
God, all of that which is a frightful burden on the shoulders
of the poor.

Jesus thus judges the tree by its fruits and like a sharp
sword he constrains us to abandon the terrain of a distant
God and the terrain of ideas on God. He leads each one to
self-unveiling: to honor God is to show that he is here below
in order to bring happiness and liberation and not up there in
order to legislate and punish. The one whom Jesus identifies
as the God of Abraham, of Isaac and of Jacob is a God who
does not deem it unworthy of his glory to soil his hands in
everyday human situations and with everyday people. And if
Jesus unhesitatingly upsets the sacrosanct Law it is because
he cannot admit its baleful applications through which hearts
are chained and oppressed. Hence all that he sees there is vile
haggling and a sham where God's pavilion is used to cover
rotted merchandise. The struggles between Jesus and the
pharisees took place on this concrete terrain to which Jesus
led his adversaries, this everyday life to which they had absolutely no desire to go, because they knew that there they
would be unmasked.

The sabbath therefore is not primarily the day of God. It is
the everyday life of men that is the locus of God, the locus of
his act of liberating love, the day in which one restores to man
his freedom. God wills that man's loaves of bread be
multiplied, that all be invited to the banquet, including
women and children (Mark 10, 10-16) who in Israel were considered as second-class citizens before the Law. It is not
primarily a question of fasting (Mark 2, 18-22) but of participating at the table of Christ and of brotherly sharing.
And, of course, it is those who lack bread and who are chased

away from the table of men who understand the language of
Jesus and follow his God. Those who fancy that they are
fulfilling the Law perfectly cannot but be deaf and indignant:
for they deplore that by his deeds Christ might shatter hierarchies and give the same place to the marginalized and to the
ex-communicated as is accorded to them, the strict servants
of the Law. They are scandalized to see him soiling the purity
of the Law (Mark 7, 1-23), they are cut to the quick in their
deepest selves when he contests their authority and their will
to power and he castigates them publicly (Mt. 23). Most surely, it is because of their utilization of God that he provokes
them and convicts them as guilty of imposture.

Thus Jesus, through his deeds and his sayings, reveals how
he views God: a God who does not respect the religion—and
the religious structure of society—such as obtained in Israel
in his time.

By virtue of this fact, Jesus appears as a subversive. But it
is because the God that he proposes is himself subversive. His
adversaries can do nothing else but reject this God who upsets
the Law and shows, by condemning Jesus, that such a God is
of no help to him and that therefore he does not exist. Jesus'
disciples, saddened after his death, saddened to see his adversaries triumph over him, a just man, are going to hear the
powerful wind of the Paschal event. Then their eyes are going
to be opened, and they will see that God has sided with Jesus
and they will understand that this God is the God of Jesus.

A God of Mercy

The terrain on which the God of the pharisees acts, a terrain of ready-made ideas, ordinances and interdicts, is thus a
terrain wholly different from the one on which the God of
Jesus acts. The pharisees fit God into the terrain of principles
and invoke the space of his commands. On the other hand,
they consider it blasphemous and despicable to involve God

in everyday life and in the happiness of human beings. Now this is precisely what Jesus does: the entire sermon on the Mount reveals this other view of God which is that of Jesus.

The "Beatitudes" are, in fact, not a moralizing discourse but a prophecy in which Jesus says who God is, and what his morals and his mode of acting are. The disciple will act "like God," he will be "perfect" or "full of tenderness" as God the Father is "perfect" or "full of tenderness." What is essential therefore is to see how this perfection of God is expressed: not in beautiful formulas belonging to the heaven of ideas, but in life, in circumstances, in the ups and downs of daily life, those of the life story of each human being and of the history of humankind.

Who then honors the God of Jesus? Here we must recapitulate the text of the Beatitudes in which it is man's happiness that honors the God of Jesus. Yes, the one who pursues the happiness of others and his or her own happiness honors this God, because this God is a God of happiness.

This lyric poem which springs up from the heart of Christ, this lyric poem of the Beatitudes is primarily a hymn to God, who is happy. He is a God who is poor, as has been so well demonstrated recently by F. Varillon in his book *L'humilité de Dieu (The humility of God)* or previously by K. Barth, in 1956, in his book *The Humanity of God:* just as we say of someone that he or she has a lot of humanity, that is, a great respect and much delicacy towards others, of God it must be said that he has this poverty, this tenderness of heart which makes for politeness, which induces self-effacement in front of the other. God created man, the Son of God became man: signs of a God who effaces himself by leaving to man his freedom.

The God that Jesus proposes is primarily this poor God, the opposite of a perverse God, lying in wait for the slightest lapse in man. Since the end of the Middle Ages and, above all, since the past one hundred years, quite a large number of theologians and preachers speak, more or less consciously, of a vengeful God who wills the death of Jesus as reparation for the sins of men towards him. Speaking of Jesus, during the Lenten season of 1891, Msgr. d'Hulst exclaims: "He is the cursed one par excellence, malediction become man! . . . God therefore began by instituting justice." In 1660 Bossuet had said: "Jesus Christ has been submerged under the redoubled and multiplied blows of divine vengeance." For them, the point is to show that God's justice must absolutely follow its course and that "his mercy was tied as though powerless," as Msgr. d'Hulst says.

Present-day preachers no longer dare to directly present this God-tyrant who has revulsed so many of our contemporaries from Roger Martin du Gard to Albert Camus, and who has forced them to take the just and honest position of a radical rejection of this tyrant and culpabilizing God. So they preach a God of mercy, but surrepticiously they reintroduce the God of justice by confining Christians in a very subtle way: they lead Christians to self-accusation and to self-culpabilization. Thus in the Lenten season of 1976, Père Bro—and he is far from being the only one—gave his fourth lecture the following title: "Mercy is more redoubtable than justice." And the full text with which he concluded this lecture follows: "Since the Passion on Mount Calvary we are invited to understand, at one and the same time, to what terrible unconscious and odious end we have come, the executioners of our brothers. Because they have forgiven us by entering into the wound of God instead of demanding that justice be done unto them, we are forgiven. Yes, let us hear all the sighs and all the lamentations that rise from this universe of nations and of the poor of whom each one of us, in his or her own way, is the executioner. Behold them, look upon them, all those who refuse to demand justice for themselves against us. Behold them and listen to them, the descendants of those, who since Christ, have chosen mercy, and behold, finally, on their faces this sole justice victorious over evil because it is born of love, the justice of those who have accepted to be with Christ in agony until the end of the world."

Thérèse of Lisieux had understood, with all her feminine intuition, that her sisters of the Carmel of Lisieux had been educated by a certain spirituality to proffer themselves to God as "victims for sinners." And by virtue of this fact, they were invited to offer themselves as victims, to place themselves above the sinners, to escape the common condition: this mode of behaviour led to a secret, unconscious but grandiose pride. It was, moreover, still another way of placing oneself on the terrain of criminal justice. And to her sisters who thus wanted the justice of God, Thérèse of Lisieux said: "You want the justice of God, you will have the justice of God. Each one receives from God exactly what he expects of him."

To ask Christians to condemn themselves, to insist that they should feel themselves as executioners, is again to place oneself on the plane of criminal justice. On the one hand, one preaches with noble words God's tenderness and, on the other, one constrains Christians, in the name of the same God whom they have supposedly relieved of his responsibility and tyranny, to judge themselves as nothings and to feel themselves as the protagonists of an agony of guilt until the end of their days and until the end of the world.

This God is not the God of Jesus, a poor God and not a judge. Here, on the other hand, is how an agnostic, Casamayor, has spoken of Jesus. In his book *La tolérance,* he writes: "One beautiful morning, on the shore of the Sea of Tiberias, someone came to say: 'I give.' " Period. The gift, gratuitousness without a counterpart and without ulterior motive. A simple idea and why not a natural one? For it has never been demonstrated that giving is not as natural as taking.

"It is at the moment of this event that the traditional societies felt the full blast of a mighty gale hurtle by, so to speak, and they wobbled. These very societies that were based on the notion of "gain" sensed the danger. They liquidated the trouble-maker, but his lesson was not lost. Not on his disciples who were eliminated or made to feel as though they had been made fools of but who, at any rate, recovered. But it was lost on his adversaries. They understood that their society ran the risk of being destroyed and they found the answer in the inexhaustible arsenal of morality. Unable to endure the act of giving without receiving—this naked, stripped, inexplicable, dangerous, explosive, fecund act—they subjected it to a sterilizing treatment. Their guile consisted in incorporating the act of giving into a judiciary system. They *judged* it and they declared it *good,* and they restored it to circulation by sticking the label "virtue" on it like the fleur de lys stamped on the backs of convicts."

"To give without receiving no longer was a general, simple, ordinary act. It became an exceptional act, it became a 'good deed.' "

Casamayor then grapples with merits with the same ferocity of the dying Thérèse of Lisieux to whom her prioress sister had said that through her sufferings she was about to acquire many of them. To which Thérèse replied: "I ardently hope that I shall arrive in heaven empty-handed." And he asks that we also follow Christ who invites us not to judge.

It is very difficult for man to acquiesce in believing this God of poverty. A kind of culpabilization, very deep-rooted in man, makes him ceaselessly re-create, in all times and in all latitudes a God-tyrant. If we limit ourselves to the Christian West, we can see this continual elaboration in a certain number of works. For example, Dostoevski. After nine years of penal servitude in Siberia, the writer was to draw from his experience and from that of the other convicts this thought: "Let us cross the threshold of the tribunal with the thought that we are guilty. May this heart-breaking event serve us as punishment. If this penalty is sincere and grievous, it will purify us and make us better."

There exists, consequently, a rage to efface the original stain, the defilement of culpabilization. When two Russians are involved in a discussion, Dostoevsky observes, one can be sure that they are talking about God or about socialism, about original sin or about liberating anarchy. And he adds that, at bottom, it's the same thing. In such a problem-complex there is a madness for the absolute, the absolute called God or the absolute called State. Before such an absolute, an agnostic of our day, Claude Roy cries out: "It is not a new faith or more faith that men would need. What is needed, rather, is to stop believing." And Claude Roy elaborates his thought: "After 1930 the Bolsheviks could spit in the face of Dostoevsky the Seer: he is their father, whatever they may say. The Father can curse them in advance: they are his children, whatever he may say. The salvation of humanity is not in the hands of believers, because a believer almost always becomes fanatic. It is in the hands of those who can hope for much without believing anything, who can act without making of their action an absolute, and who mistrust drastic remedies because the fate of human beings is at stake. The world needs the lukewarm who want to give it warmth, doubters who do not doubt that progress is possible, unbelievers who believe that one can and one must always try. It needs iconoclasts and not idols. It needs minds who finally will stop playing heads or tails with the absolute, between siding with the Revolution and crying out that if God does not exist everything is permitted. It seems to me quite probable that God does not exist: it is precisely for this reason that everything is not permissible. It is not because Christianity or Islam are spiritual religions that they are perhaps a little less harmful today than the great temporal religions of State: it is because they are weary religions, because they vented their spleen in the persecutions of yesteryear, crusades of old, the Inquisitions of times past."[2]

Dostoevsky is, as Claude Roy says, "the apostle of holy suffering and self-flagellation." And he concludes: "It is not only from despotism that peoples must be liberated, but from the unconscious fear of freedom."

Man has no greater anxious desire than to find someone forthwith to whom he can transfer this gift of freedom which the unlucky creature brought with him upon being born. Dostoevsky is the prime illustration of this anxiety. He never ceases from wanting to "transfer" to a theocratic emperor or to an autocratic Church this freedom in which he saw man's bottomless depths. His genius, his delirium, the suffering of the innocent convict and the humiliation of the "liberated" subject, remind us that humanity must be healed not of the disease of atheism but, to the contrary, of this kind of neurosis that indefinitely creates gods, that transforms all its projects into proclamations, all its purposes into idolatries and all its enterprises into religions.

"Humanity must be healed from Dostoevsky, the Russian, the one *who knows*, in order to find again the universal Dostoevsky, the one who doubts, the one who accepts himself as a doubter, for *harmony costs all too much,* without consenting to accept misfortune as an element of harmony willed by God."

Another agnostic, Phillipe Vianney, clearly shows the political incidence of this God of culpabilization. For some time this God has been utilized by the Right: "Yesterday Pétain exploited the remorse of the Right: France was a sinner and her misfortunes were a just punishment."[3] But Vianney shows that this same God can be lived on the Left and by Christians too. "Certain Catholics or moralists of bourgeois Christian origin are sowing remorse on the Left: because in their eyes their class and the Church have been guilty for centuries, indeed for two millennia. They feel enjoined to exhort, to judge, to punish, hoping thereby to redeem themselves. They want to win over the Left to their cause as they did, not without courage but with a lyrical excess, during the Algerian war. They have already broadly succeeded and are the present-day motor force, relieving Sartre of what could be called the culpability of the Left. Will Mitterand, basing himself on genuine lay-persons, be able to exorcise France of this culpability, the burden of which risks compromising his victory?"

"The culpability of the Left? Its forms are multiple and the whole exudes a feeling of boredom and sadness that prevents creative action. Authority is always suspect, but it is impossible to oppose it, to say no to it. Individual responsibility does not exist for young people, women and the economically disadvantaged. There are only social causes underlying theft, violence, despair, drugs.

"On the other hand, the employers are always guilty which dispenses one from seriously inquiring into the real causes of the perversion of social mechanisms and from proposing new definitions and realistic game rules. The justification of everything and of all action is an almost neurotic need. It is sometimes shameful and always suspect to defend French interests on the international plane, except against America viewed as the source of all evil.

"Europe is an imperialist idea and the white world must beg forgiveness. It is inconceivable to oppose communist force in regard to which one feels a visceral weakness, just as it is bad form and absurd not to refer to Marxism. Caricatures? Moldy reactionary smells? The examination, at any rate, is necessary because the conditioning is deep and there are dramatic precedents. The Left disposes of an unlimited capacity to adopt dogmas, just as the Right ceaselessly recreates its myths and its hatreds."[4]

In conclusion, Vianney asks that we go beyond "the bad conscience" and he proposes for political work and progress that we make a genuine "joy of living" the subject of an experiment.

A Vulnerable God

When preachers, those of yesteryear or today, when writers like Dostoevsky propose an absolute keystone God—and that can be done just as well under the sword of the truth that one says he possesses or under the cover of mercy which becomes "redoubtable" like a cleaver, like a court sentence—we understand, that both of them want, like the pharisees of Jesus' time, to impose a God who assigns them this authority—moral, political or spiritual—over others.

By virtue of this fact, we can understand the resistance Jesus encountered when he proposed the God of the Beatitudes to the people, the opposite of an absolute. For he said: "Be happy" to the crowd, He invited them to dare to believe that God is Tenderness and Happiness in himself first and foremost and for all men. He invited each one to be poor of heart, to be open-handed, not to exhaust himself in the search for first place, the first places are always bitter, He invited each one to tell oneself that one never arrives, and thus to be young today and still remain so tomorrow.

He invited us to be gentle, tenaciously gentle, and to be strong on this score so that we are blithe about being taken in by those who believe they are stronger, to go beyond the needs of useless and pointless revenge and aggressiveness, to be tender towards others as towards oneself.

He invited us to be able to weep, to let ourselves be moved, to have a vulnerable heart like the heart of God himself, to protest with horror against the slaughter of innocents, to cry out like a madman, as a prophet and as a living being in the face of evil, suffering and death.

He invited us to have a hunger and thirst for justice, to invent just relations with others as partners who mutually recognize each other, to communicate unaffectedly and with pleasure, to have a passion for dialogue with others as with God, to live the principle that it is just to be grateful towards all those whom we meet because we always receive from others.

He invited us to tenderness, to a heart that is stirred here and now, that leaves the past to the past, that forgets the wound received formerly and gives the oppressor another chance today. And, perhaps, a friendship then can be born between the former oppressed and the former oppressor.

He invited us to have a totally purified heart close beside which others find freshness and breathe freely, a heart that loses no time in moralizing, that dares express the impulse of affection that it feels springing up in it, a heart that does not primarily refer to interdicts.

He invited us to struggle for peace, to create it day by day, to act while being oneself disarmed, to transform the stiffest hostilities and the most twisted oppositions into true bonds.

In the Beatitudes Jesus proposes to men the very portrait of God: a poor, gentle, vulnerable being, enthusiastic for true dialogue, for just relations with each other, a being that is ever new, capable of making a good of evil itself, creator of peace. Therein lies the "perfection" of the God of Jesus; it is not the monolithic "perfection" of omnipotence lived for itself or of impassiveness, but "perfection" in the opening to others such as God is himself in the Trinity.

Chapter 5 of Matthew which is a commentary on the Beatitudes is a pressing invitation to love that life, such as it exists in God, to be "perfect" in the manner of the Father, according to that perfection, the perfect opening.

This "perfection" is the "salt of the earth." To seek another kind, according to which one seeks oneself, renders one tasteless. On the other hand, it is a matter of loudly proclaiming this paradoxical perfection, this opening to others, this vulnerability: such is the light that must be shown as much as possible to all, a light that is not shown in words but through deeds (Mt. 5, 3-16).

To be in keeping with God's justice, that is, in keeping with the justice of his being and of his heart, these deeds must go deeper than those "of the scribes and the pharisees" (Mt. 5, 20). Their justice confines itself to "You shall not kill." But the God of Jesus goes much further: there is a way, more subtle but just as effective to kill the other by ostracizing him or her, by ruining his or her reputation, by making him or her appear to be a fool. This, too, is murder, as grave as physical death (Mt. 5, 27-28).

No longer is it just a question of not committing adultery. According to the God of Jesus the point at issue is not to want to possess a woman. Jesus knows very well to what degree a look can be predatory, the masculine look most particularly. He demands this real poverty that consists in not appropriating to oneself a woman, not even through a look. And thereby he touches on the deepest recesses of the heart, the will to power and possessiveness (Mt. 5, 27-28).

Likewise, it is necessary to go beyond the law that permits one to set aside his wife with a writ of dismissal. We cannot reject, at our pleasure, the other with whom we have bonds of marriage or of friendship, like an object become useless. Jesus does not want one to repudiate another, to kill another by a unilateral act of dismissal (Mt. 5, 31-32).

The God of Jesus does not admit oaths, whether they be true or false. Oaths are like swords of Damocles that we suicidally make hang over our heads, stupid procedures of self-alienation that prevent life from pursuing its course, of renewing itself. What is essential is to say "yes" or "no" in the very moment, to live in the everyday circumstance: there is no need to conjure up the future (Mt. 5, 33-37).

There is a strict justice that enjoins that one apply an exact balance, a *quid pro quo:* vengeance must be proportioned to the offense, no more no less. Jesus upsets this balance. For he knows that the accountancy of vengeance never ends: after an offense and a vengeance, the offender who has been punished always deems that vengeance has been excessive in relation to the offense and that he must re-establish equality anew. It is tantamount to escalation, whether it be between individuals or nations. Jesus wants to shatter this escalation through a strategy of non-violence, which is an enobling action for one who dares to live it. It is an action which, moreover, is a form of wisdom: to put up a step by step resistance to a paranoic merely nourishes and re-inforces his illness. There is a way of non-resistance that is a victory, a manner of cutting things short in relation to certain rights that is a gain (Mt. 5, 38-42).

The conclusion that Jesus draws after evoking this whole new style, this new way of life, is the following: the point is not only to love those who love you (a flat, spiritless tit-for-tat balancing of accounts), but to love those who do not love you. This is the manner of God who loves those who do not love him ("the evil, the wicked"), he greets them each morning with his sun and causes his beneficent rain to fall on them, they are served as much as the "good." This manner of being of the God of Jesus, liberal and open-handed, goes beyond a narrow conduct, flush with the ground. Jesus finds that such a new manner of being is worth trying (Mt. 5, 43-47).

The first Beatitude shows the spoliation of self. Only the relation remains. After there is nothing: God has only himself to give.

It is here that we can confront the God of Jesus. For Jesus, what is essential is not to say "Lord! Lord!," but to say: "God exists, I have met him!" Jesus does not pose the question: "How prove the existence of God?" Jesus makes no peremptory affirmations on this matter and he does not begin to philosophize.

What interests Jesus, what pleases him, what enthuses him, is God's manner of being, his comportment, it is the manner of acting of this God with whom he feels to be in a very deep, very particular bond. It is, if we may put it so, experiencing God day by day, God in human history. In Jesus' time, the whole world admitted that God exists: the pagans in their way, the Jews in theirs. Rare were those whom the Bible called "fools" who said that there is no God. They said that, moreover, because they found that God was too absent, that he barely manifested himself. And, in fact, they were symmetrical to the pharisees: like them, they judged God on the basis of his efficacy—or his inefficacy—on the basis of signs that he gave or did not give. Both sides aimed at the image of a utilitarian God—or of one who aroused no interest.

Jesus does not prove the existence of God by proving that he is useful and efficacious. Of God, Jesus points out only that he is unpredictable, that he intervenes where one least expects him to and does not intervene where the religious authorities assign him residence. Jesus takes a kind of mischievous pleasure in drawing God's countenance in terms of unpredictability and unexpectedness: this countenance does not express itself primarily in religious rites and signs, in the temples atop the mountain between heaven and earth, it expresses itself in the deeds of everyday life, the most tenuous, like the widow's mite, incognito, like the welcome extended to "the least" as recorded in chapter 25 of Matthew. After Jesus one can no longer talk to an efficacy of God that is precisely measurable or that can be made magically and surely to come to pass. It is not, says Jesus, because you belong to the people of Israel or because you are of a strict religious and moral rigor that you are unfailingly chosen by God or the object of his interest: it so happens that the publicans and the prostitutes will precede you, and why not? God is gratuitous, his sun shines on all, his strength of love is given to all, without distinction—so much the worse for these jealous ones who are the older brothers of the prodigal son. To speak of the efficacy of God is to depict him as an accountant who dispenses his favors in a calculating way, with generosities or restrictions according to the degree of adherence to him, with precise balances of rewards and punishments. God is not efficacious, he is of a total gratuitous liberality, he gives without calculation, and with profusion. No good marks or bad marks. And it is this infinite openness of God, this unmatched magnanimity that interests Jesus, this, as it were, "immoral" and "unjust" God who gives as much to the laborer of the eleventh hour as to the one of the first hour: is that not scandalous at first sight? But this totally liberal attitude of God—the opposite of the "God lying in wait" of Mauriac, a Jansenist God who waits for you at the bend of the road—this attitude delivers captive souls, hearts that feel crushed by the lack of love, the lack of opportunity. No longer can one think that one has been excluded, that one is a non-chosen, that one does not have "baraka," that is, God's blessing.

It is no longer a question of leading a life in which the essential would consist in accumulating merits and of standing out more conspicuously than others: all are admitted and loved.

It is very difficult to admit that all are loved by God, this God who liberally welcomes everybody who has feelings of extreme kindness for all and each one. One would like to be outside the common herd, a privileged being, a son of aristocratic family set aside and bearing the mark of a great name. Yet the God of Jesus is people, in the sense that all human beings are admitted by him, he believes in all, including and primarily, the least and the last, those whom men normally reject: the sick, the poorly dressed, the poorly nourished, the wretched, the unloved. And the apostles, after the resurrection, see that he has placed in the first rank the one whom the religious authorities of Israel had degraded to the lowest rank as one ex-communicated, a pariah, one crucified outside the holy city, not even recognized as prophet and stoned as such.

The history of unbelief, since the death and the resurrection of Jesus, is primarily the history of the Church herself, of resistance to this particular God. When Congar says of the Church that she is indissolubly "saint and sinner," he is pointing out that the Church is born and continues to be "saint" in that the apostles and the Christians in their wake have perceived the God of Jesus: Jesus himself, the Father and the Holy Spirit, in that the Church does not cease, in the depths of her being, to live this reality that she, too, has recognized. But, at the same time, he is pointing out that the Church is "sinner," that is, frequently incredulous, unbelieving in relation to this God. The history of the Church is yet to be written most particularly as a history of her continual resistance to this God, as the history of a stubborn unbelief, of the "sin" against the Spirit.

Most often, in fact, this history of the saintliness of the Church, of the moments when she acknowledges this God has been written not in the moments when the Church was temporarily conquering somebody, but in those moments, for example at the time of Francis of Assisi, when the humble people and the mystics, all those who truly believe in the God of Jesus, succeed in making a kind of cultural revolution and with their living wave wash over the harsh rocks that fancy themselves as the sole witnesses of God, smug and proud witnesses to boot.

But the history of the Church's "sin" of unbelief has hardly been written. One author[5] devotes the third part of his book *Dieu selon les chrétiens (God according to Christians)* to a description, in nine paragraphs, of *Dieu selon les siècles* (God according to the centuries) from the primitive Church to our days. His intention is to show that "the history of God is not solely a theological history . . . It is primarily and before all else a cultural history. Hence also a political, social and economic history. The coutenance of God depends on

the shiftings of the culture and of social groups more than on
ecclesial vicissitudes."[6] This is an interesting approach, but
should not one go even further? The problem does not lie
primarily in an opposition or in a dilemma between
"theological history" and "cultural history." Before posing
the question in these terms, it is necessary to show the history
of the faith and of the unbelief of the Church, the history of
the opening of the people of God, of its welcome of the God
of Jesus, *at the same time* as it is the history of the rejection
by this same Church, of her resistances and misunder-
standings, of her deviations and oppositions in relation to the
God of Jesus, in short, the history of the Church's sin of
unbelief. If the apostles, in the Gospels themselves, have not
hesitated to record the history of their incredulities in relation
to Jesus and, therefore, to the God of Jesus himself, why
should the Church refuse to preserve the memory of her sin,
of her sin of unbelief all through the centuries? The apostles
followed Christ with many blundering steps before the resurrection, but they also proceeded with great caution after it,
even though they had received the plenitude of the Holy
Spirit. The Church has the promises of eternal life, but she is
not the good God and she moves forward along a difficult
path—the Christ did not die so that the open sea to which he
had invited her would be a great calm and a life unbuffeted
by winds and storms.

We may wonder why so well-informed an author should
have thus omitted this history of the Church's sin of unbelief.
There is the fact of contemporary unbelief—never before has
there been in France such a large number of men and women
who answer "no" to the question: "Do you believe that God
exists?" And we can see, through the poll conducted by *La
Vie* in 1967 and 1977 in which it posed this question to young
people between 15 and 29 years of age. It disclosed a shattering acceleration of this negation: in 1967 16% had declared
that they did not believe in God and ten years later the

number of non-believers rose to 30%. This incontestable and very important fact of a clear declaration of refusal in relation to the proposition "god exists" must not, however, mask a question still more important for Christians, namely the following: "You, Church, you, People of God, what do you say, going centuries back in time and today, of the God of Jesus? How do you view him? How do you translate his comportment? How do you show him?

It may be that many young people of today want no more of a certain God such as Christians have defined him in the course of the centuries and whose contours they continue so to draw today. And at this moment they are not necessarily unbelievers vis-a-vis the God of Jesus but merely reject a certain countenance of God transmitted by many Christians, a countenance that no longer has very much in common with the true countenance of the God of Jesus. It may be also that, among young people, others are really unbelieving vis-a-vis the God of Jesus, that is, they have perceived, through Christians or otherwise, that he actually exists, and they refuse this God of Jesus, this God of tenderness and universalism.

But then the primary question is to scan the real identity of the God of Jesus. After which we will be able to see how, in the course of the centuries, the Church has been "saint and sinner," how she has manifested and masked this real identity. Perhaps the aforementioned author would have been able to provide a better study of it if he had not discussed the "parameters" of faith in God according to Christianity only in the third part of his book, and above all if he had begun from the beginning by reading the history of God through the centuries and in the Church starting out from the essential light, that furnished by Christian Duquoc in his book *Dieu différent*:[7] the trinitary figure of the God of Jesus. It is a significant fact that H. Bourgeois speaks of the Trinity only as a seventh and last "parameter" of the Christian faith, after the culture of an epoch, the ecclesial experience, the knowledge, the difference between God and men, evil, the non-believers. And still he speaks only of the "trinitarian sense" and on a single page. This is an error of perspective as distressing as that of Cardinal Garrone who, twenty years ago had published for the good Christian people, a *Panorama du Credo*,[8] in twenty chapters in which there was no mention of the resurrection. Yet, H. Bourgeois had glimpsed the essential, but in a hesitant manner and without at all being explicit: "The ups and downs that the trinitarian sense had known in the course of centuries are probably very significant of the countenance of God in different epochs."[9] It must be confessed that this "probably" is not without a touch of wit.

A God in Communion With Himself

The God of Jesus and his Church has a trinitarian countenance. The primitive "images" of God, such as they are reflected in liturgical practice, for example, are distant. The first "formularies" of the faith "incorporate three elements: the fatherhood of God, the event of the Christ and the gift of the Spirit."[10]

Under the pressure of Greek objections, the Churches had to borrow a philosophic language in order to establish the non-absurdity of this Christian manner of presenting God. This effort was necessary, but it has rather strongly damaged the primitive trinitarian images. Is it possible that our epoch, whose culture is marked by so many images, will turn its gaze toward these primitive images?

What transpired in the first centuries of the Church? The theologians underwent, at one and the same time, the influence of the biblical universe and of Greek thought. The Christian community refused to cast a slur on the monotheism received from Jewish Scriptures, but it maintained the trinitary countenance of God which, in the eyes of Israelite and later Moslem believers, seemed to damage monotheism.

In order to defend themselves on all these fronts, theologians proposed explications of the trinitarian countenance through the prayers we express in worship. St. Augustine speaks of the comparison with the family where there is father, mother, child. But other theologians conceptualized to excess, and this led Christians to consider that this trinitarian countenance had no real bearing on their life. In this conceptualization, the presentation of differences in God was expressed against a backdrop of unity. There was a kind of great fear among theologians as well as Christian people, of dealing with the preponderance of the divine Absolute, of the One.

Yet, it is on this point precisely that we Christians must reflect further, abandoning this terrain of fear before a certain feeling of the divine that forces upon us a constraining unity. The Christian faith from the outset clung to the notion of maintaining differences in God. It has underscored that the Father, the Son, the Spirit were not interchangeable but, rather, that each had a manner of being, a comportment proper to him in relation to us and in themselves. If there are no differences, there cannot be a true communion, a true communication among them. Each one exists only in his relation with the others. None is an *in himself,* a kind of "bachelor of the worlds" of whom Chateaubriand spoke in order to designate God.

Here we are now moving into a problem fundamental to the humanist culture: unity is perfection, whereas difference is viewed as weakness. It is in this way that one proposes non-difference as an ideal, and that we want to reduce everything to equalness and selfsameness and that the message of Jesus, which puts emphasis on difference, "Love one another," is denatured into "Love yourself in the other." It is thus that one wants to make priests, lay-persons, monks, that is to say holders of "the one" who suppress difference—sexual difference, for example, because this sign of sex underscores difference, lack and limit. Nobody can at once be man and woman. In order to suppress this difference that provokes scandal one reduces everything to masculine perspectives for example. And it is thus that one has established hierarchies of value, challenging equality which is not the reduction to selfsameness but the promotion of differences: each one has a right to be unique to the world, no one must perforce enter a unique world. And it is thus, in order to secure the unique omnipotence of God, that one has presented a self-sufficient being closed in upon itself.

Yet the Spirit shatters this fenced-in state, he shows to what point God is the one who shares, opens himself to differences. The God of Jesus Christ is not uniquely the Father in a face-to-face with his Son which would lock us up in the narcissistic desire of a face-to-face with God. He is just as much Breath, outer energy, constant creation and renewal. One then turns one's back on the inner-directed, self-centered God of theism, a seducer of men whom he draws to himself and whom he leads to merge with his motionless beatitude. The God of the Christian faith is movement, emergence from self. He has a taste, an attraction for human beings, he is interested in their differences. This God is not a god of death who obliges man to repetition, to reiteration, to an incessant march in the selfsame ruts and the selfsame identities. By virtue of this very fact, He is our opening to the new and He is creative presence.

IV

GOD
TODAY AND TOMORROW

In 1869, at the time of the founding of the Metaphysical Society, Thomas Huxley proposed the word agnostic in reference to the apostle Paul's allusion to the altar dedicated in Athens to the Unknown God (Acts 17, 23). In 1884, Jules Clarette used this expression in speaking of agnosticism as the "doctrine that declares the absolute to be inaccessible to the human mind." He added that almost all educated England was agnostic, rejecting in principle the torment of doubt. And the philosopher M. Caro cited even some wives of agnostic pastors. Thus it was at the century's end that this characteristic attitude of agnosticism sprang up in which people no longer felt obliged to pronounce some belief on the subject of God's existence or non-existence.

God Unknown

To be sure scepticism had existed for centuries. In the 4th century B.C., for Pyrrhus, founder of Greek scepticism, and for his pupil Timon, all things elude both certitude and judgment. Pascal was to make frequent use of Pyrrhonism which served him to show "man's weakness." Indeed Pascal states, "We do not consider philosophy worth an hour of trouble . . . Pyrrhonism is right." In the *Pensées,* scepticism has the apologetic function of humiliating and degrading human knowledge. But it was Montaigne, an excellent authority on ancient scepticism, who was mainly responsible for Pascal's "Pyrrhonism." Montaigne considered the human being incapable of going beyond the singularity of his impressions and of constructing any kind of universal knowledge. If he himself, as he said, is "the subject of his book," it was because for him, any datum is relative to a particular, situated being.

In the 19th century and today, Pyrrhonism blossomed into a practical philosophy under the name of positivism. The idea of relativity, the Einsteinian critique of the notion of simultaneity, moreover, restored a new vigor to Pyrrhus' ancient relativism. Our epoch very keenly feels the historically relative character of institutions and morals, of languages, and of civilizations. In dogmatic answers it often sees the source of fanaticism and evil.

In France the great exponent of agnosticism was Littré. In his youth—as he himself affirms—his beliefs had been those of deism: God, the soul, immortality. He had derived these beliefs, without any dogmatic influence, from the milieu around him. In his youth, like Pascal and Jouffroy, he had experienced "his night." But, contrary to Pascal, this "night" made him lose his deist beliefs (just as Jouffroy had lost his religious faith in the night): one night, secluded in his room, he began to study when suddenly he asked himself on what basis "he believed what he believed." He found no answer to this question. Thereupon "he completely dropped natural religion and became a denier, in a manner very much like that of the 18th century." "But denial, like doubt, obsessed him.[1]

The generation of 1850-1860 was characterized by the love of science and trust in its methods. Comte's positivist doctrine, the philosophical transcription of the scientific movement, was to be essentially propagated by Littré. Yet, in 1875, when Littré was received in the Grand-Orient of France, at the moment of his initiation into the Masonic order, he was asked to respond to the following question: "What are man's duties towards God?" The text of his speech reveals Littré's agnosticism. Here are some extracts:

"Those who know positivist philosophy, those who have

read some pages from my pen, know in advance what I am about to say, awaiting neither an affirmation nor a negation. 'What do you mean by that?' This will be the objection of the greater number to whom the principles of this philosophy remain unknown. 'Is it possible neither to affirm nor to deny?' Yes, that is possible and, in our point of view, that is wise, that is salutary.

"These absences of affirmations and negations, fragmentary to be sure, and which none hitherto had thought to assemble, have been arranged in an hierarchical order by positive philosophy. And when it thus held them under observation, in their totality, which embraces the knowledge of the world, of man and of societies, it enunciated that the total doctrine resulting from their partial doctrines affirmed nothing, denied nothing concerning a first cause or a supernatural order.

"Whereas Christians damned their pagan forebears, and revolutionaries despise their Christian forebears, a greater and better recognition embraces the entirety of the human past. Nothing is to be divided in the immense heritage that has been transmitted to us. It is neither a question of showing a deep piety for our ancestors nor of showing a deep concern for their descendants, when dogmatic prejudices classify men not according to their services but according to their beliefs.

"Whoever declares firmly that he is neither a deist nor an atheist makes confession of his ignorance concerning the origin of things and concerning their ends, and at the same time, he humbles their haughtiness. No humility can be deep enough before the immensity of time, of space and of substance that is offered to our view and to our mind, before us and behind us. In the presence of these distant horizons discovered by science, I do not hesitate to repeat the mighty words of Bossuet who, enraptured by an unlimited contemplation, although it was one of a wholly different kind, exclaimed: "Be silent, my thoughts!"

Gabrial Marcel, at the beginning of his *Metaphysical Journal* (1914-1923), defends himself against the charge of agnosticism: "That there is no such thing as a last word on things or, at least, that this last word cannot unhesitatingly take the form of truth, and that the fundamental value of religious life consists precisely in that it transcends, in some way, any enunciation with an objective aim bearing on the universe—are, it seems to me, the leading ideas of the first part of this journal. It would be erroneous to see in it a roundabout form of agnosticism. The agnostic remains this side of a certain truth that remains unformulatable only for him, because the conclusions to which human thought is subjected prevent him from ever breaking the circle of phenomena."

One of the heroes of Paul Bourget's novel *Nos actes nous suivent (Our acts follow us)* defines himself as follows: "I'm what the positivists call an agnostic," and this means as he goes on to explain, "we cannot know either causes, nor substances, but only phenomena."

The term was admitted all the more because of the cachet of England that surrounded it and, as Anatole France said in *The Revolt of the Angels* (1914), "he was agnostic, as one says in the fashionable world, so as not to use the odious term of free-thinker." Paul Claudel, as a poet, put together three terms that he found equivalent "agnostic, positivist, materialist" (*Un poète regarde la Croix, (A poet looks at the Cross),* 1938, p. 16).

In *Augustin ou le Maître est là (Augustine or the Master is there,* 1933), Joseph Malègue wrote: "Agnosticism is the only solution to problems in which givens are lacking." In this novel, which describes peasant and intellectual France between 1880 and 1914, Malègue clearly portrayed the crisis of faith in the face of agnosticism.

On the philosophical plane modern thought is very marked, as is known, by Kant whose positions are based on two postulates adopted by many of our contemporaries: on the one hand, the only givens that are offered to knowledge are phenomena and, on the other, the knowing subject has no other contact with the real save through the intuition of the senses.

All this is translated into an opposition to metaphysics and by an anti-dogmatism that often assumes the countenance of anti-intellectualism. One denounces discourse—often with lots of discoursing. And, above all, one hurls oneself into action by rejecting all reflection, by choosing the "lived" against reason. Intelligence, which is a function of man, is minimized and despised. Fideism, consequently, becomes then the objective ally of agnosticism: "The Faith," writes Maurice Clavel, "will not establish itself until it purifies itself in particular of all metaphysics . . . I want to cleanse the Christian religion of philosophy."[2] And Clavel does not hesitate to affirm that if fideism is not the whole of our faith "it is at least a necessary factor of it, and perhaps the prime one."[3]

And the religious indifference that characterizes so many of our contemporaries, is most particularly in the line of agnosticism. In other times, not to concern oneself with the question of God, to consider that there was not even a need to pose the question was an exceptional attitude. Charles Maurras, more than fifty years ago, wrote about a young Pole, Charles Jundzill, whom August Comte had welcomed like a son and a privileged disciple: "Not only was God absent in his mind but his mind also felt, if one can put it thus, a rigorous need for the absence of God."[4] This attitude is a common one today: it is lived quite naturally as a dictum of scientific progress.

This indifference is not a form of laziness, it is before all else a mentality, an experience at the core of which the religious dimension finds no place. But this attitude is born of an implicit affirmation: that the question of God need not be examined, that it is of no interest. For how many of our contemporaries, including believers, does the fact that God exists or not change anything in history or in the daily life of humankind?

This indifference is not a superficial expression but the reflection of a global situation: it is an historical phenomenon. The laws of political, social economic life are based on precise principles before which belief proves to be a force of little weight. Everything happens as though beliefs did not exist, or almost so. The inefficiency of Christianity, for example, becomes more and more an affirmation of right based on the autonomy of the secular order and, in the final analysis, on the autonomy of man, the author and norm of history.

Thanks to science, to technology, to social action, the role that God played in the world is from now on being performed by man and in a manner that is surer and more efficient.

A Post-Atheism

By virtue of this fact the atheism of the future is a post-atheism: it no longer is manifested through committed and militant denials but by more peaceable forms, forms that are rather disconcerting inasmuch as they express an exact balance between "yes" and "no," that is, agnosticism. Vatican Council II had particularly attached itself to the Promethean forms of atheism, to atheist humanism. However, since the '60's, agnosticism is the intense explosion of this post-atheism. And this brief dialogue in Julian Green's novel *Chaque homme dans la nuit*,[5] published in 106, is quite symptomatic.

" "I have become a complete agnostic."

"In fact, you mean that you're an atheist?", asked Wilfred with a knowing air. Angus took a cigarette from his pocket. "It's much more subtle," he said snapping his silver lighter. "I deny nothing. On the other hand, I assert nothing positively. Do you get the idea?" "

It is in this ensemble that we must see that the question of God henceforth is being posed in an altogether different way than formerly. For a long time an intense polemic had developed between the exponents of theism and those of atheism: both were brotherly enemies who argued in a symmetrical manner and nourished each other. What the former affirmed, the latter denied, and vice-versa.

It is interesting to read a page of one of the great present-day theologians—who later became cardinal Archbishop of Munich—a page which, written in 1968, clearly shows the changes of perspective. In fact J. Ratzinger therein speaks of the Christian as follows: " . . . he who takes his calling seriously will clearly recognize not only the difficulty of the task of interpretation, but also the insecurity of his own faith, the oppressive power of unbelief in the midst of his own will to believe. Thus anyone today who makes an honest effort to give an account of the Christian faith to himself and to others must learn to see that he is not just someone in fancy dress who needs only to change his clothes in order to be able to impart his teaching successfully. Rather he will have to understand that his own situation is by no means so different from that of others as he may have thought at the start. He will become aware that on both sides the same forces are at work, if in different ways.

"First of all, the believer is always threatened with the uncertainty which in moments of temptation can suddenly and unexpectedly cast a piercing light on the fragility of the whole that usually seems so self-evident to him. A few examples will help to make this clear."[6] J. Ratzinger then cites the example of Thérèse of Lisieux. But then our theologian symmetrically depicts the unbeliever's position: "If on the

one hand the believer can only perfect his faith on the ocean
of nihilism, temptation and doubt, if he has been assigned the
ocean of uncertainty as the only possible site for his faith, on
the other the unbeliever is not to be understood undialectical-
ly as a mere man without faith. Just as we have already
recognized that the believer does not live immune to doubt
but is always threatened by the plunge into the void, so now
we can discern the entangled nature of human destinies and
say that even the non-believer does not represent a rounded
and closed existence. However vigorously he may assert that
he is a pure positivist, who has long left behind him supernatural temptations and weaknesses, and now accepts only
what is immediately certain, he will never be free of the secret
uncertainty, whether positivism really has the last word. Just
as the believer is choked by the salt water of doubt constantly
washed into his mouth by the ocean of uncertainty, so the
non-believer is troubled by doubts about his unbelief, about
the real totality of the world which he has made up his mind
to explain as a self-contained whole. He can never be absolutely certain of the autonomy of what he has seen and in-
terpreted as a whole; he remains threatened by the question
whether belief is not after all the reality which it claims to be.
Just as the believer knows himself to be constantly threatened
by unbelief, which he must experience as a continual temptation, so for the unbeliever faith remains a temptation and a
threat to his apparently permanently closed world. In short,
there is no escape from the dilemma of being a man.''[7]

Thus the question changes as question, and this modifica-
tion is one of the most important mental mutations of our
time. Under which influences and through which paths? For
the past twenty years sociologists, ethnologists, mythologists
have discovered, in the ensemble of their searchings and of
their inventories, that there was an order, a logic running
through these strange matters. Men fashion myths to regulate
their exchanges: exchanges of words or of goods. This ex-

perience of exchange suffices them in itself, without a need to have recourse to a transcendence. Hence the investigators reveal that the myths and the religions have sense contrary to rationalism and atheism that assert the incoherence of the religious discourse and haughtily dismiss it. But they also dwell on the self-sufficiency of these myths and find that theism goes too far in adding a supersense to sense. Quite a few philosophers also lend a hand to muddying the quarrel between theism and atheism: Heidegger, for example, who sujects the idea of God to a very keen critique, saying that we raise a relative term to an absolute. Heidegger refuses to grant consciousness permission to traverse this passage to a summit and, instead, would have it acquiesce in an abyss: one cannot utter the ineffable, and theism is wrong for wanting to attain it. But atheism is wrong to reject the notion that there is in man a gap and a sense of the unfathomable—there is a "suspension of thought" . . . .

If now we return to the question of God, in a more existential sense, what can we say?

It is known that Gide was fond of repeating that it was extremely difficult to prove that God exists and even more difficult to prove that he does not exist.

Many Christians are believers who would prefer that God's existence be immediately given like the conclusion of a logical demonstration, with irrefutable proofs. For them faith, based on a solid rationality, would follow later. Thus the first stage would be knowledge and reason, the second stage would be faith, that is, recognition and trust. Yet Christian faith cannot develop in the wake of reason, as if in the baggage of a victorious army and its triumphant proofs. It is in the selfsame moment that the believer places his trust in God and that he sees that his act of trust has something of a rational character. It is in the interior of the experience of faith that the believer knows that faith is not absurd.

At the same time, the believer perceives that his experience of faith cannot be purely and simply an act of his brain. His faith is the concern of his whole life, the totality of his being is involved in his faith, with his temptations and his quests, with his mode of thought and his ways of acting, with his social situation and his historical vicissitudes. He sees clearly that he must live out his trust in God in everyday life, a trust that each day is reflected upon, that each day confronts questions, that each day is threatened and deepened further.

Agnosticism accordingly has transformed many summary views held by Christians who have too often confused their faith with a certain way of vigorous assertiveness—"iron-clad belief"—a way of turning one's back on reason and of humiliating it. In France the simple faith of the charcoal-burner, *"la foi du charbonnier,"* has become proverbial to signify an unquestioning, unconditionally accepted faith. We should like to join to this expression another proverb: *"Charbonnier est maître chez lui,"* the charcoal-burner is master in his own home, in order to express the idea that the "simple faith" is the faith of someone who intends to be sure of himself, master of his choice and who is certain with a sovereign certitude, namely, that the faith is his business, that he has examined it in all its facets and that he is the master of it, like he is master of his property, his home.

Today charcoal-burners are a vanishing breed and the "simple faith" makes place, happily, for the faith of the nomad—or of the pilgrim, or the traveller, as one may wish. Faith no longer situates itself in the constraints of a voluntarism or of proofs that are once and for all defined and stratified. To be sure, it has a stake in the will and in reason, but it is in a constant movement of confrontation with doubts and with a deepening process within itself. It must go from the oasis to the desert and from the desert to the watering-points. It is a personal decision made "in one's soul and consciousness," of course, but it situates itself also, and just as much, in a companionship: faith can no longer be the sole splendid isolation of a being immersed in his or her devotions, it must be confronted with experience, with the words and with the deeds of other believers.

The Human Gap

Today's believer finds himself confronted by a new awareness; up to now he had believed more or less confusedly that he could demonstrate that atheism is impossible. He knows today that one cannot refute anyone who has opted for the non-existence of God. Atheism is neither rationally demonstrable nor refutable.

How then does the atheist—or the unbeliever—of today, the one who in his own life has convictions other than the Christian faith, other choices, other trusts, appear to the Christian?

But first of all it must be stressed that for this man the ultimate questions—those posed by Kant, for example, those questions in the depths of all human beings whether they be committed to causes or solitaries, intellectuals or illiterates—remain under a double heading: What can we know? Whence comes man and whither is he going? Why this world-there? Why is there something and not nothing? The second heading is the one concerned with doing: what essentially is man to do? Before whom is he responsible? Why love? What's the use of living? What is the meaning of death? What is the meaning of suffering? What must we do for man's future?

Today's atheist, very strongly marked by his atheism, poses these questions to himself against a backdrop of radical relativism. His horizon makes him see these questions as indefinite, which, in the final analysis and at the end of his journey, admit of no possible answers.

The believer then tends to say, as does Hans Küng in his book *On Being a Christian,* that the atheist exposes himself to a danger if he reflects deeply on his position: "the atheist is also exposed quite personally to the danger of an ultimate abandonment, menace and decay, resulting in doubt, fear, even despair."[8] Compassion for the atheist is not hard to come by.

Indeed the Christian increasingly runs the risk of finding himself before these new atheists for whom, precisely, the "danger of an ultimate abandonment, menace and decay" forms part of the human condition. And in the view of these new atheists, it is a form of cowardice or of weakness to want to escape this feeling and this human condition by leaning on "something stable in all change, something unconditioned in all that is conditioned, something absolute in the relativizing experienced everywhere."[9] Some decades back, the Christian willingly based himself on an apologetics of efficacy, such as charity or service, according to which Christian faith would permit Christians to live values that non-Christians did not exercise as much. Today, the Christian has suddenly perceived that many non-Christians are just as devoted to the service of others as Christians—and this, without basing themselves on Christian morality and on the God of Jesus Christ. Likewise one runs the risk of steering a false course by dwelling on the "fear, even despair" that accompanies the new atheist: the latter assumes responsibilty for the consequences that are inherent in his position. And it is here that we must measure the change of mentality that has taken place over the span of the past hundred years among our contemporaries.

This mentality does not deny all the immense contributions of science over the last century. And it is enthused over the recent discoveries of science, particularly in the sphere of the brain. But at the same time this mentality accords an increasingly greater importance to a dimension other than the positiveness of science and of rational proofs. It discovers in effect in man and his destiny an unclearness, an irrationality, an unknowableness, a hollowness. The ensemble of artistic productions, for example, particularly over the past twenty years, expresses this cry of the human being of today who wants to speak of the unclearness of all the realities, of the wound that it discovers in each one of them, of the shadow zone that exists in any discovery—even in the greatest, and even in love.

Consequently the "danger of an ultimate abandonment, menace and decay" with its train of doubt, fear, even despair is not perceived by many moderns as a mortal danger which must be escaped at any price or as an abyss that must be filled, but as a fault, a break in continuity, that prevents man or society from closing in on themselves, a fault through which one perceives a certain light.

What the Christian tends to regard as "a negative thing," as a danger for man, many of our contemporaries choose to see as a happy vulnerability, a *felix culpa,* a happy fault—in the non-geological sense of a lack, a failing—through which man gives up his narcissism, his inner-directedness and opens himself to others, a fault through which he escapes from the walls of the gulags within which his unwarranted certitudes might confine him.

How to make this enormous slippage of mentality understandable? Freud asserted that the two poles of life were love and work. We have lived a whole period of the history of humanity, above all in the West, in which work has been predominant. And all the more so because we wanted to fill the abyss of doubt which is the question, the space of love. How many beings have immersed themselves in work in order to avoid confronting the problem of "loving," in order to avoid immersing themselves in this mad adventure that genuine love is. But a day comes when this question of love, long set aside and repressed, rises again to the surface and forcibly and urgently imposes itself.

The same applies to faith: Christians had posed it in terms

of work, of will, of production, if not as merchandise—and of a bargaining with God. Yet Christians are experiencing, and will continue to do so henceforth, the shock of what our society itself is experiencing: the return of love. Faith, for that reason, can return to its original space, which is not primarily a space of work but a locus of freedom, a relation of love. We must try to delineate exactly this new space of faith which, moreover, properly fits into a good biblical tradition.

In the face of the question: "Does God exist?" the classic procedure in philosophy is to start out from the "starry sky above our heads": one tells oneself that this world has a cause and that therefore God must exist. Or still one starts out from "the moral law that is found in our heart" and consequently the point of departure is a certain presence of God within ourselves. And after having thus asserted God's existence one tries to list, as well as possible, the qualities of God such as can be attributed to him without falling into too human, too simplistic a view. Finally, one tries to discern how God can work in our world and be in relation with men.

But there is a manner of proceeding other than the strictly causal way. It is that employed by biblical tradition, it is that perceived in a variety of ways by certain contemporary sciences. Here it is matter in effect of a union contracted through mutual commitment that presupposes from the start a law, a contract: each one of the two parties has rights and duties and each one is recognized in his identity as long as he respects the contract. Hence the contract is a collective act which is primary, which establishes the individuals—it is not the individuals who are primary. Each individual must recognize that a pact precedes him, as the mother tongue precedes his word—it is not the individual who creates his mother tongue, it is the latter which constructs it, that gives it a backbone. And in a pact, the individual is obliged to recognize that a force transcends him, that he is enjoined to observe certain rules, that he cannot be his own father and that, in the final analysis, he must give up that notion as lost.

But this is not only a case of the law that interdicts. A pact is at the same time an opening on the future, a promise, a hope. When someone has recognized that he is not the master of his birth and that he has received his existence from others, he can set out on a path towards a goal. This goal is the relation, a relation as such with others, without appropriation, for possession would slow the march forward, destroy the movement, abolish the hopeful expectancy. This situation is ceaselessly ambiguous: the human being would often prefer to possess himself of a more absolutist course instead of remaining open to the relational.

It is here then that the experience of love takes its place. It is an experience difficult to understand because the habitual rule of our human societies is the marketable value, the give and take, production, exchange, posts, the social hierarchy. Yet love is a *gratuitous* relation as such, useless from the point of view of "production"—which is not to say that love does not bring a dynamism.

Love is gift, a gift that none of the two partners can control, it is sharing, encounter, feast, a hospitality.

To enter into a mutual recognition is to enter into the language with all that it signifies of loss. We wanted to be exactly present to ourselves as in the maternal womb, imprisoned with the mother. We wanted everything and at once, to have this totality immediately. When we enter into a pact of mutual recognition, we lose all this, we give up our lures. We perceive that it is not we who can create love, that it is given to us gratuitously. Then we discover that we have it not and that we are not, and yet that we can in all freedom share in a common work or feast what we are not, and reciprocally make ourselves "the gift of nothing," the gift of our reciprocal poverties.

We can find ourselves before three different ways of recognizing God. The first is very inadequate. It is that according to which we recognize God as the one who gives the Law, as a power who protects and who, in the final analysis, rewards by protecting the life of the one who follows his commandments. In fact, this is in part true: the law protects the child, obliging it to live by preventing it from remaining attached to the maternal orbit, forbidding it acts that would be dangerous for it. And it even protects men against themselves: were it not for the interdiction to kill, an escalation of violence would break out in which each one would risk losing his life.

But man perceives that he remain mortal, even if he scrupulously observes God's law. Man sees that he does not escape death and that the calculation according to which he had wagered on the law and on God in order to escape death fails, in the final analysis. The law appears in the end to be inefficacious. At such a moment he brings about a reversal: he perceives that the law is not only weak but that it is crushing, that it prevents him from flowering. Thereupon he revolts against it and rejects the "legislator-God." He feels like a camel carrying too heavy a burden and he shakes it off.

Hence the law offers only a relative protection against death and, finally, it is death that has the last word. Man then seeks his answer in a different way. He sets out on a quest to confront death, to dare death. If death is unavoidable, man nevertheless can skirt around it in part. For example, by creating a descendance for himself or by creating works of art through which—as his children and as masterpieces—he will be able to pass beyond death. Or else by creating "singing tomorrows," that is, the best possible living conditions for those who will follow, seeds of life for the future. Here, the forces of life struggle against the forces of death, man plans and carries out projects, risks his life and, at times, he loses in order to gain something beyond death.

Man, at such a moment, tries to recognize a God who is a living force, an impulse for those projects that try to conquer death. God becomes the creative energy that works in all men and in all humanity in order to bring about the advent of justice and peace. God is consequently the Meaning, the one who gives to the life of a human being its unification.

Yet, when a man who has thus recognized God as a "moving force" meets others who have no need whatsoever of a reference to God in order to establish plans and to bring their plans and their struggles against death to a successful issue, this man poses a great question to himself: did he not himself produce God as the term of his projects? The God recognized as the energy, support and end of our actions is still an impasse, like the God of the Law, who was the "stop-gap" of our failures and of our new condition for living. God cannot be recognized as anything other than what he is. And he has nothing else to give but himself.

God is not a "giver" who would be painted incognito into a corner of a painting by the artist. God does not give man security or assurance, rules of behavior or parapets. God wants, and wants only, to give himself. We cannot avail ourselves of him in order to escape death or in order to build a world to come. We cannot hold him prisoner of our dreams or of our ideals, even the most sublime. For the reason that he is Gift, we cannot possess him. But we can receive him and we can give to him.

For several years now, people have been talking of the poverty, of the vulnerability, of the tenderness of God, of his sadness, of his unusual and unexpected ways, of his absence. Formerly one stressed his omnipotence, his strength, his greatness, his wisdom. One would discover him, undoubtedly through the facts of life and the crises of history. One wanted to find him through a certain feeling of his presence. There has been an immense progress, a renewed awareness of what the true men of faith in all times have always perceived—namely that one could not appropriate to oneself The One who is Gift. And many ardently desire that this awareness become global, that it no longer be the insight of a few but of the whole People of God, in its totality.

God is better discovered as a "gentle breeze." Claude Vigée, who has convictions other than those of the Christian faith, once told a group of Christians: "I shall simply recall to you this, in the name of a tradition that is not mine, but fundamentally yours: in the first *Book of Kings,* the prophet Elijah on the mountain of Horeb, no longer knew how to reply to the questions: 'Where is God?' Do I have faith?" that you are discussing. There was a thunder, there were many mighty natural phenomena, an explosion of light, an earthquake that followed a mighty wind—but it is not there that God is. He is neither in the lightning nor in the thunder. Elijah finally arrives at a cave in which there is nothing save what the Hebrew text calls—and this is what Elijah perceives—*quel demamah daqah,* that is to say, the voice of the gentle silence, the voice of the gentle breeze, which is like an emanation. It is there that God is, in this voice that we almost never hear. Those who have not heard this voice, those who have not wanted to hear this voice, those who have not walked long enough on the mountain of Horeb in order to find the right place, those who have not had the experience of the still small voice of silence—or that of its emanation or taste, it's the same thing—those persons *must of necessity* be agnostics. They must wait, and remain waiting even if it be for a whole life-time, or as the Talmud teaches, for several life-times, one after the other. There is nothing else to say on these matters.

" 'Is this waiting hope,' 'Yes, it is hope, it is honest agnosticism.' "[10] God is always but barely recognized, as though inadvertently, indirectly. God lets himself be discovered only from a back view—"God created man like the oceans created the continents: by withdrawing" (Honlderlin). God does not cease to withdraw. Not because of sadism, but in order to tell us that we must not confuse things and the Gift that he is and in order to invite us to ceaselessly go forward: for we will never have finished with love. God reveals what Love is as pure loss of self, as total gratuitousness. God is poor, as Jesus said: for thus does he speak of his father in the very first beatitude.

God of The Future
or, the Flight Forward

Many Christians may be disconcerted with this presentation of the Christian faith—a presentation that in itself is not new and whose expression is just the biblical datum. That cardinal Ratzinger should write that the believer cannot exercise his faith save on the "ocean of nihilism, temptation and doubt" seems to be an unheard reversal of what people ordinarily believe. At the same time this notion of faith against a backdrop of absence and darkness, this approach to God as the one who is "gratuitous," who is beyond the useful and the useless gives rise to strong doubt and many misgivings. We tell ourselves that such a presentation of God is dangerous because it is demobilizing, and that it invites all those who are militants and who want to create a new world to lay down their arms. This God of gratuitousness, assimilated to a God of the feast, seems then to be a God for those who have leisure time and who make no effort to change this world in accordance with ideas of the partisans of justice, harnessed to the task of achieving a better truth and a better organization of human social relations.

This rubric of a God of gratuitousness, who in this case may seem to be reduced to a God of the superfluous, easily falls subject to the criticism of those in the Church who are more conservative and want to stress the image of a God who governs and dominates the order of the world, a God who predestines and foresees all, who has established a nature of things that must be followed point by point. For them God is the guarantor of order.

In both views, God is primarily a God who acts, who ordains, in the two senses of the word. In Jesus' time, the Zealots, who thought that their hands were armed by God in order to revolutionize the world, and the pharisees, who were self-assertedly the spokesmen of an order foreseen by God, were in accord with each other in the matter of mistrusting the God of gratuitousness of whom Jesus spoke and in the matter of discarding and trying to kill, finally, this presentation of God.

Both sides, in fact, find it extremely difficult to abandon the convergent images of God that they always have in the depth of their being: namely, the idea of a power, a reality that makes things change in one direction or another—and in the direction, of course, which one hopes they would take, a reality that punishes or rewards the stance or the steps taken by this or that individual, this or that group, a reality that comes to the aid of our failures and our purposes, collective or personal. God is then not much more than a Destiny who irrevocably fixes the course of events or who gives them the requisite shoves so that they are tipped in a precise direction—which amounts to the same thing.

This notion of a Creator or Destiny is a typically western notion—and we are speaking here of believing as practised in the western world of today. There is in this world a will to fashion the universe, to guide the universe with an iron hand and to do this by means of slide-rules and by laws that allow nothing of an indeterminate character to get by, so as to arrive each day closer to overcoming the uncertain, by rendering everything accountable and by reducing everything to measurable productions.

This has led to the apex of our current western

technological revolution: data processing which on the one hand is composed of computers and, on the other, of data. These data consist of all that which can enter into the memory bank of the data processing system. It then becomes a matter of codifying all things in such a way that they can, having become quantifiable, enter into the computer's memory bank.

It is thus that one wants to create history, knead it, arrange it, foresee it, and that is in effect to destroy it. But if we look at it more closely, the manner in which some want to see God as the one who foresees all or who makes everything happen according to their heart's desire, this manner of viewing God involves wanting to create a supreme computer that digests and imposes everything. We know that in the work of the computer, in the end, we find only the imput. Many believers, at some moment in their lives, perceive that their God is a computer which they have built with their own hands and which does only what they want it to do. God, then, is only a copy conforming to themselves, to their view of the world and to their idea of themselves.

This creation of a useful God, fashioned by the hands of man, has existed at all times in the western world. But it has been singularly highlighted in our day because of the situation obtaining in our epoch. In previous centuries, and only some decades ago, the men of the western world, whether Jews or Christians, had in effect a stabilization which gave them the certitude that their God had duration, and that their civilization, in his image, also had the assurance of permanence. Hence no questions were posed respecting the future which could be viewed only as an indefinite reproduction of what was in the process of living in a stable and permanent way. The handful of adventurers or marginalized beings who did not share this certitude were properly repressed and flung back into the darkness of ignorance or of illuminism.

Today when the future has become an interrogation of the present, when we are no longer certain that the future will be the same as the present, we would like all the more to master this future which, as we can clearly see, eludes us, and the more we fail in our efforts to foresee it, all the more do we want to program it. So we draw up prospectives, forecasts. Like the title of a book by François de Closets, we draw up "Scenarios of the Future,"[11] we want to discern the contours of the year 2000. Yet, in this book we can see that the particular purpose is to make hypotheses in regard to that which most of all eludes our control: violence and happiness, freedom and health, all that which up to now it was impossible to feed into the computer's memory bank. How can we fail to perceive that these *scenarios of the future* are related to Utopia.

Gilles Lapouge, in *Utopia and civilization,*[12] has well defined Utopia, this notion that had been vegetating for a long time and that for the past twenty years had been undergoing a luxuriant explosion, indeed a wild proliferation. He distinguishes four forms of Utopia. The first form of Utopia, that of Plato, Thomas More or Cabet, is the conception of an ideal city in which everything is minutely foreseen, planned, organized, a city which is a self-winding system of clockworks in perpetual movement. In such a city, the individual and his freedom are suspect because they constantly menace the exact order of the whole. The good citizens are those who belong to the city by performing the functions that have been assigned to them and that make them contribute to the excellence of the machine, with punctuality and precision.

When we perceive that this Utopia in its first form, mathematical and architecturally exact, we rub our eyes and tell ourselves that it was not in this sense that one normally viewed Utopians. The latter had appeared to us as unforseeable and whimsical beings who did not lock others up in a closed system but who on the contrary lived in the imagination, on the fringe of society. They were viewed as gentle dreamers. In fact, alongside the utopians properly so-called, who are great systematizers, there are utopians who are against systems, the utopians who extol whim, freedom, vagabondage, the "Do what thou wilt" of Rabelais and of his Abbey of Thélème. But we can see that these second utopians can almost also be as constricting as the first: for example, in the face of the first that, on the plane of sexuality, regulates love and procreation, the second, that leads to promiscuity and laxism, also tend to impose norms and to want everybody to be a naturist and a swapper. The second utopians have no regard whatsoever for the group, for regulations, for organizations. Nevertheless their ideal of freedom can, subtly, become a new stifling law and therefore, while purposing to establish personal freedom, they can make their freedom weigh heavily on that of others.

God In Danger From Beliefs

In a time like ours, uncertain of its future, utopians of the first or second group will gladly lead us in directions that they have all too well foreseen in order to sweep us along with them. They are both symmetrical to each other. They respond to a very strong need of people today, namely to the need for beliefs. A poll conducted by SOFRES in June-July of 1977,[13] at the request of the Rosicrucians, showed that of all the French, men and women, who were queried about their need, if any, of an ideal, 28% declared that they were just as much in need of an ideal at the present time as they had been before, but 45% affirmed that they no longer needed one. Only 16% of the respondents felt such a need less than before. Agnostics like Claude Roy are crushed by this "need to believe" which is taking more and more people on board . . .

If our contemporaries listen to the siren voices of the utopians, it is because their voices take them out of this today for singing tomorrows, and out of the horizon of this limited present for one that is limitless and radiant. Our time is hard to cope with and many would like to escape it to become beings outside the world and outside time, to destroy this present-day society and start out again from zero.

The last page of the magazine of the Moonies in France which is called *Le Nouvel Espoir (The New Hope)* always carries Malraux's phrase: "The 21st century will be religious or it will not be." In the aforementioned *Scenarios of the future* by François de Closets, one chapter deals with religion. It is striking to see that the two currents in it are sketched in relation to the future of religion: one asserts that the religious sentiment is dying out before science and rational knowledge and the other states the very opposite, that God is not dying, that faith has a future and that, moreover, the death of God had even been discerned in previous centuries and that the obituary was false, unfounded and premature.

Both currents pose as champions of the future, as utopians. They take positions, in a radical or fideistic manner, but always as utopians according to the ideas that they form of the future, of the establishment of this or that, according to their convictions.

We can see the danger that God, so to speak, is running into. In our time when the future is uncertain, God is viewed as uncertain by a greater number of our contemporaries. In order to mitigate this danger, I wonder if the proper method is to want at all costs to utilize the most powerful and the most sophisticated of the modern media in order to affirm that God will exist, that there is a future for Him. There is a gentle manner, all the stronger, of believing in the future of God: hope. Hopefulness has an altogether different depth than the quest for compact certitudes. When we see the enormous success, in 1978, of a peremptory book on *Life after life,* we can measure the giddiness of our contemporaries and their quest for such certitudes: this brings us ever closer to what Feuerbach rightly called "the believing unbelief of modern times."

To be sure, those who assert that God has no future are subject to an unwarranted dogmatism, as much as those who contend the contrary. And by virtue of this very fact they provoke the escalation of the "belief" in a future for God. In other respects it is absurd to appear to sweep away the past of faith and even its present, as do some who assert that God has no future. Reviewing de Closet's book in *La Croix,*[14] Guissard writes: The future will register mutations that affect religious institutions: who would doubt it? It cannot establish that the religious past of humanity will one day be considered as an episode devoid of significance save as a wrong turn or as a detour leading to a finally triumphant scientific truth.

"Above all it has no business to allege that in this very moment the deeds of faith, the lives that have staked all on faith, the coexistence of the religious man and the man without God, this immense geography of the divine on the western, Asiatic and African earth, the human beings in search of a meaning that they do not find in scientific reading, or that proclaims itself as such, of the universe and of its terrestrial elements, all count for naught."

To place oneself thus on the plane of the defense of believers and of their authenticity is not the real problem. It is still a matter of wanting to assure ourselves that the future has some continuity with today. And bishops and popes, consequently, will always be able to reassure themselves by noting the quantity of the faith of the past and the great number, even today, of adherents to the Christian faith.

Is it not a matter furthermore, as Guissard witnesses in the conclusion of his article, of wagering on the fact that man will hardly change and that the religious sentiment will remain? "The year 2000 is only a short distance away from us. Too short a period between now and then for God to be buried and a certain type of man along with him. Later, much later, in order for the deicide predictions to come true, it would be necessary that the future change man, the incorrigible explorer of the mystery of his depths. One can accept the wager that such a change will not occur. Or are we preparing for men who would no longer be like us? God alone knows?" To be sure, we can gamble on this fundamental dimension of the human being which is the desire to explore mystery. But will not man be offered a certain number of other "mysteries" to discover—the mystery of his brain for example—which will turn him away from the mystery of God?

The believers of the Bible were tempted to model images of God in wood, clay or iron. For several centuries now, modern men have dealt with the temptation of making God no longer of materials but of ideas in order to fabricate their idea of God. Is not the new temptation that of forging a God with the future, with utopia? When we note today that so many young people are abandoning the Christian faith, or becoming indifferent to it or turning away from it, we must go to the very end of this observation: they do not want a God of the past, marvelous and folkloric. But neither do they want a God of the future who would enjoin them either to genuflect before him to save the wicked world or who would bring to fulfillment a new and perfect world.

The point then is not to succumb to the fascination of the "future of God" utopia that is being championed by voluntaristic affirmations. At the same time, in regard to the man evoked by Guissard as "an incorrigible explorer of the mystery of his depths," it is a matter of knowing that this quest of man does not guarantee a future for the Christian faith as though it were a certainty. For several years now Christian hope has often been presented in the way the "simple faith" of the charcoal-burner was proposed before and one bases oneself on the future by drawing a draft on it, as it

were, in order to void the precise questions that are being posed today. This is not much better than a flight forward, a way
of conjuring away present questions.

If we reject being reassured cheaply with mortgages on the
future, we find ourselves before a problem that many
agnostics pose to us. For example, Claude Roy who asks
himself about the "simple faith," *la foi du charbonnier*, ever
being born again in the heart of man and ceaselessly taking
on new forms—as we have just seen in our day with the wager
on the future—poses to himself and to us the question of the
"need to believe" which is a global phenomenon. "The
phenomenon of faith, of the *wanting to believe* in the domain
of religion or of religiosity (examples: the religious
renaissance in the countries of the East, the frequent passage
from genuflecting before Stalin or Mao to a 'religious'
spirit—the typical case being to mention minds as radically
different as Alexander Solzhenitsyn, Lezlek Kolakowski, or
Roger Garaudy).

"It would be necessary to analyze the forms of religion
without faith and those of faith without religion, to show the
complexity of the correlations or of the radical distances between the experience called mystical, or of the sacred and the
theologies. There are religions without God and almost
without dogmas and, inversely, dogmas without religions.
There are atheist mystics and anti-mystical "believers." And
there is, stubbornly inventing for itself an object ceaselessly
replaced, the simple faith of the charcoal-burner, the pig-
headed need to believe."[15]

Such an unbeliever emphasizes the relativization of beliefs.
A. Grjebine shows that "an increasing number of individuals
find themselves deprived of what up to now had been their
principal reason for being: the quest for substance and for
adherence to an unquestioned conception of the world."[16]
What we are living though, "the re-questioning of the domi-
nant moralities and religions" strikes him as a very rare

phenomenon in "the history of civilizations." And, "the obligation to choose their beliefs 'relativizes' each one among them."[17]

Another commentator stresses the necessity of belief and the "vital necessity to leave everything to a great man or to a system."[18] "It is necessary that a function of the ideal, positive or negative, be maintained at whatever price. This ideal can be incarnated, if one can so express it, by no matter what, as with the fetichist. There is no need for a great political doctrine. Any 'signifier' can turn the trick. Even a dead one (look at all the mausoleums). It will just be more active. God has known that for a long time."[19]

Another agnostic, Christian Zimmer, connecting moreover with Cardinal Ratzinger's opinion, dislodges us from our ways of basing ourselves on the past and on the future. "What is at the heart of faith, if not an essential doubt. The simple faith of the charcoal-burner does not exist: I believe because I doubt, and I doubt because I believe. Doubt here is at once fundamental and ungrounded. It is necessary because it hollows out the absence in which desire dwells. And belief, finally, appears only as the fine point of this desire. There is no belief without desire, consequently without a lack, without the absence of the object.

"Hence there is nothing as fugitive, as unstable, as fragile as belief. Nothing less compact, less homogeneous. Nothing less tied to time, so menaced by it. It is in this sense, perhaps, that it maintains a privileged relation with the narrative, the 'fictional' narrative. The latter is not bound to produce stimulants of beliefs, but stimulants of desire that become desires to believe. In that case, whence comes this desire? What is the countenance of this will to mask the lack, to fill the absence. This dogged denial, this refusal to see what I must not see? This capacity to give myself *freely*—at least in appearance—to an illusion? Is it the triumph of the pleasure principle over the reality principle?"[20]

We constantly want to escape the night, the darkness, we want to be approved by God, to hold him, in final analysis, between our hands. Jesus' disciples, before Easter, had also tried to obtain the first places in his Kingdom, to be well-established, to have a power as solid as a rock. Yet their paschal faith sprang up, precisely, from the void before which they found themselves, from the false images that they had fashioned of God and of the future, from their images of the power of God and of their own power.

Our faith is similar to that of the disciples before Easter, if it is a recourse in the face of situations that seem insoluble or of questions without an answer. For faith does not come to give us tools for the transformation of the world and God is not a maker of these tools. It is man himself, with his own hands, who must create his tools and forge his history. The disciples had to pass through the paschal night and in the passage they were liberated and rendered capable of accepting a reality that is not made of the blood and sweat of men. It is not possible to encounter God without passing through such things. We cannot open ourselves to God except at the end of this tunnel. Such a passage in which one is liberated from oneself for the encounter with an Other, is the complete opposite of a demobilization: the disciple who has passed through Easter is all the more returned to the fetters of the world in which the injustices and the obscurities are stronger, in order to break them.

This passage is a painful parturition, there is nothing that smacks of a feast about it. To acquiesce to the God of gratuitousness is to renounce this images, the utopias that had primarily sustained us in the first steps of faith, it is to walk on the sea. In this difficult walk, we meet the One whom we did not expect: we had seen him differently, we did not believe that he was thus. Happy are those who believe without having seen. To believe is to recognize The One whom we had taken for another, The One whom we had not seen at first—like Mary Magdalene who, on Easter morning, saw a gardener, and she experiences a terrible moment during which she perceives that her heart, however loving, had not recognized Christ, during which she perceives how she still remains egocentric in wanting to retain for herself the one whom she had now clearly seen but in whom she did not yet profoundly believe. One must die to oneself, and radically so, in order to be in a position to be deprived of support and in order to gratuitously accept, without counterpart, the God of gratuitousness.

The apostles lived this death. They had staked all on Jesus. This man so incarnated their hopes! The disciples of Emmaus tell their fellow-traveller about the collapse of their dreams of the future that they had shared with Jesus. They recognized him only at the moment when he disappeared (Lk. 16, 31). As long as the apostles knew who he was, as long as they pinned labels on him: prophet, miracle-worker, messiah, their eyes remained closed. As long as we still think that we know too much about God's identity, it is impossible to recognize him.

WHAT BECOMES OF VALERIE?

The other day I saw Valerie again. She brought me, among other things, a poem written by a contemporary. Here it is:

> "You must not doubt
> the one
> who tells you
> that he's afraid.
> But you must be afraid
> of the one
> who tells you
> that he's a stranger to doubt."[1]

In an article in an issue of *Concilium* (No. 106) devoted to young people and the future of the Church, Père Congar, evoking the crisis of the Church, situates it within a context: "The crisis is so acute, so impossible to master, only because it proceeds from the fantastic mutation of civilization with which the world is now familiar, a mutation of an amplitude, of a depth, of a generality, of an extent and of an acceleration such as to render it without precedent. Everything is being questioned at once, all that which has been received from the past. Everybody is shaken by it but young people, apparently, more than others."[2] Young people do doubt, but with some sense of awareness, they look their fear in the face.

Rupture and Parturition

In this same article Père Congar shows how the transmitted faith is not only that of Abraham, Jesus, the Covenant, but that it is also that of dogmatic formulas, of codes, of structures of authority: "The Church has thus clothed her heritage with a culture: an admirable creation, full of genius, of a profundity, of sap and of poetry."[3]

But Père Congar adds: "Tradition is not only transmission: nothing would be *transmitted* if it were not *received*. What would be the "tradition" of the Eucharist to a population in a language that it could not understand?"[4] "Tradition is reference to a depository, it is also life, history, growth . . . Let us recognize that we have dwelt unilaterally on the first aspect."[5]

In the exhortation to Evangelization in the modern world, Pope Paul VI has said: "The rupture between the Gospel and culture is without doubt the tragedy of our epoch." It is this tragedy that we must examine together. For if we love the Gospel, we cannot but be saddened at heart to see this rupture such as the Pope sees it, such as we see it in the daily life of our contemporaries. And if we try to reflect on the new cultures that are being born today, on the values that they convey, it is, to be sure, because we belong to our time and we cannot ignore what is being lived here and now by many of our contemporaries—a "lived" in which, moreover, we participate more often than we think. Hence, it is better to try to take account of it. But if we pursue this reflection it is, strongly, with a view to the Gospel: "Woe to me if I do not evangelize." When we try to live the Gospel, it is like a blazing fire that is in our heart and we would like it to spread. We are not, and we know this well, creators of the faith or transmitters who would be handing down something to which they have proprietary rights, something which they fashioned with their own hands. God alone is the source of faith. Only the Spirit of the Risen Christ can make us participate in the trinitarian communion and make us express in truth: "Abba, Father." But we must work, like the Apostles, to tell the world of today of the new existence that is the Risen Christ, to make known as best we can, with the aid of the Spirit, through the languages of the men of today, the nature of this new existence that transforms all being, all mentality, all culture. The apostle Paul has talked of this new existence as of a "new birth." We desire that our world of today enter into this new existence, that it be born in Christ. At the same time, we must take part, each one of us, in the work that the Holy Spirit is accomplishing even today. In his analysis of the conciliar constitution *Dei Verbum*,[6] G. Defois has shown that the model from which it draws its inspiration is perfectly vertical, that the transmission of the Word of God is effected from summit to base without the least intervention of the People of God. The latter has only a passive role, it is not an outstanding party in the act of tradition. This is a conception that is bound up with the conception of language as pure instrument. And the Word of God thus is an "elsewhere" that falls from on high with no relation to history and to the society in which it springs up. A conception also bound up with the altogether pyramidal conception of the Church, the Church being a mass determined by its apex, authority having, by degrees, taken priority over the content of the truth that the Church has received the grace and mission to preserve and protect. This model has in part broken down to the advantage of a communal conception as in the early years of the Church. There is a greater recognition of the primacy of what is transmitted over the transmitter. And there is also a recognition of a consistence proper to the language—it is no longer only a matter of having a correct language, outwardly orthodox. This fits in with the stance of young people who want to believe and not merely glide into the world of another. The problem: how reconcile free creativity and adherence to a millenary content? How live, at one and the same time, a constituent faith and a constituted credo?

Let's Become Bilingual

We can say that this quest for an active reception of the Word of God is positive in itself and that it responds, moreover, to the need for creativity that is one of the essential marks of modernity.

In order to carry out this work to which we are enjoined, this "mission" demanded of every Christian by Christ himself, we must constantly, and first and foremost, have in our hearts and minds the expression of the faith such as the primitive community, the redactor of the gospels, has transmitted to us: we must scan the gospels in order to understand from within what the gospels tell us, in their language. Although it had been decided very early, under Paul's pressure, that the ensemble of the religious customs of Israel would not pass into the Church of God, the Scriptures have remained in the Church. And the Church, always in the light of the Risen Christ—it was in this light that the gospels were written—ceaselessly finds in them illumination for her experience.

But it is today that we are living, it is today that we must evangelize. The men and the women that we meet are no longer the Jews and pagans such as Paul met. They have their values and we recognize that these values, at times different from those lived one or two generations ago, are the ones that aspire to be evangelized: that is to say, not to be destroyed in the encounter with the Gospel, but enkindled by the life of the Risen Christ. *Ignem mittere in terram.* This is not a matter of genuflecting to the world, but of a confrontation with it. As Paul VI says in his testament on the subject of the world: "Let no one believe that one is doing it good by espousing its thoughts, its customs, its tastes, but, rather, by studying it, by loving it and by serving it." Yes, the point is to understand the world, to love it to such a degree, to serve it, to espouse its particularities, to become bilingual.

A Certain Rejection of Evangelization

To say, like the Pope, that "the rupture between the Gospel and culture is without doubt the tragedy of our epoch, as this was also that of other epochs," is to place, among other things, the emphasis on one fact: we are living in a time that is experiencing a great cultural upheaval. Who would dare to deny it? It is important to know that there are in our epoch such and such well-established cultures. It is even more important to see that all the established cultures are experiencing a shock, that they are being called into question, passionately defended by unconditional exponents and passionately contested by unconditional opponents: all signs that they no longer are self-evident structures, taken for granted.

And if this upheaval exists, it is not in terms of a gratuitous death instinct, or through the agency of a method called *tabula rasa*: even if it is desired to effect a *tabula rasa* in the intransigent and totalitarian manner, for example, of the young present-day masters of Cambodia. If the precedent mentalities are being re-called into question it is because of a positive desire, already existing, a desire that has been in a process of slow, subterranean elaboration in the past decades and that now outcrops in our humanity, a desire to live "differently." Certain "traditionalists," in a hermetic way, reject this fact of a present-day cultural upheaval. And they do so in the name of the faith, deeming that since the faith can not be altered, the cultures through which the faith has been expressed can not be called into question. But there are other traditionalists, more subtle, who consider that nothing can be said yet of these new cultures, of this future. Hence if we acknowledge them, we would be condemning ourselves to an incapacity to further proclaim the Gospel since these cultures are not yet formed and solidly existent. A strange position indeed, because the upshot would be to proclaim the Gospel only to centuries-old cultures, those that have proved themselves, and which would oblige us to renounce proclamation of the Gospel to the men and women of our time who are experiencing new aspirations. This constitutes a radical infidelity to the Gospel, to the first message of Christ which enjoined his followers "to teach all nations." Did Christ say that it was necessary to teach only ancient, well-established nations, and that it was necessary to keep nascent nations, new cultures, the "barbarians" outside the proclamation of the Gospel? This is to fall woefully short of the universalism of Christ's message according to which all men, all nations have the right to know that they are all loved by God. These "ferocious and sad guardians" of the Church, as Msgr. Etchegaray has described them (*La Croix,* March 19, 1977) thus succeed in chaining evangelizers to the past, and in preventing the evangelization of today. They confirm an observation of François de Sales: "Fear creates more evil than evil itself." Where, then, is the open sea, the "go forth" to which the Christ invites, the hardihood and boldness of the Apostles?

The Church Needs the World

In the preface to the *General Catechetical Directory* (Rome 1971) Cardinal Wright underscored the following: "The human themes that one can treat of (love, war, justice, peace, culture) do not enter into catechetics only by virtue of examples having a pedagogic value. They form part of its very content, to which the Word of God must bring its illumination." Along the same lines, the Synod of German Bishops in 1974 demanded that "religious instruction refer to the situation of the pupils, that it pose to itself their questions, that it seek to know their problems and that it strive to gather experiences."

To better understand this "novelty," we have in other

respects to make everybody help us, without distinction. No. 44 of *Gaudium et Spes* clearly points out to us that unbelievers themselves or the adversaries of the Church can bring "a non-negligible aid to the ecclesial Community." We receive much from our non-believing brethren who reflect, who deepen—may I pay homage here, for example, to a man like Alfred Grosser,[7] and it is so astonishing to see how a Christian, Noel Copin, interrogates him. Not to let ourselves be taught by those who know our epoch, to reject their perceptions quickly becomes, if we stubbornly persist in this position, a sin against the Holy Spirit, a lack of love of our brothers, the men of today of whose tendencies, quests and discoveries we permit ourselves to be ignorant. We can ask them for a drink just as Christ did not hesitate to ask the Samaritan woman, a schismatic, an excommunicated, for a drink. The Church has a message to reveal to the world, yes, but the Church needs the world. She needs the means that the world gives her in order to proclaim her message. "She needs the world, its language, its culture *in order to understand herself* and at the same time in order the better to open herself to the novelty of the Gospel."[8] Culture is the very place at the heart of which man accedes to faith and must devote himself to express it. The Church cannot let herself be heard by the world if she does not listen, if she does not hear the Holy Spirit in the questions, hopes and anxieties of the men and women of this time, if she is not in solidarity with a world that also constitutes her. "It is by mingling in the world with its tumultuous novelty that the Church can make a return to herself and discover the novelty of her Message."[9]

Here's Valerie Again

Throughout these pages we have never lost sight of Valerie and the mutation of her epoch, our own.

Some will then pose the question: Is the new mentality

favorable or, on the contrary, not too permeable to the Christian faith? It's a bad question because this mentality, as such, is not yet a philosophy. It is a manner of living, it is a "culture," not primarily in the humanist sense of this word, with all that it represents of values and of norms, but in the sense of an ensemble of symbols that permit social practices (production, work, politics, education etc.) to communicate.

For Valerie it is an obvious fact that we are all marked by a culture, immersed in a culture. One day she told me: "We can't do anything about it, we're born into an ensemble, we're born into a 'collective unconsciousness,' we participate in that which others have lived before us, we're fashioned by their language." Young people today are trying to live the faith, knowing instinctively that any expression of faith is marked by a given culture, that Jesus himself spoke in Aramaic. Those who come to tell them that there is a specific "life" of Christian values which, as such, show that one is Christian risk being laughed at: these young people have seen these values called Christian lived by others who do not want to talk about them or who have never heard talk about the Christian faith. From now on the exponents of the new mentality oblige their contemporaries—and among them Christians—to talk about such matters; one must be able to clarify one's position, one must express from the start from what cultural ensemble one enunciates the opinion that one is enunciating.

Likewise we can no longer *say* God at random. If I pronounce the name of God, Valerie will say—and any young Christian or any young unbeliever participating in the new culture will say the same: "Just what does that mean?" Instinctively, there, too, there is a recoil before this name which one perceives has been the object of an immense inflation, and which has "served" many: it has "served" private and public interests, tastes for domination of all kinds. The integralists always hark back to a magic phrase: "Speak to us of God." Père Bruckberger in an open letter to the cardinals after the death of Pope Paul VI, published under a bold heading in the *Journal du Dimanche,*[10] wrote: "Fathers, give us a pope who speaks to us of God." Which is spelled out in the article to mean: a pope who is not politically engaged, who is above the fray, who rejects liberation theologies, who is "transcendent." What is presented here is a God outside of man, and a man who is primarily a soul: the man presented to us there is a disincarnated being: "True, there is a Third World: many among you belong to this large portion of humanity which still suffers misery and hunger." I am sure, however, that the cardinals of the Third World understand this word of the Gospel: "Man does not live by bread alone but on every word that comes from the mouth of God." Even for them the worst of famines is that of the soul.

Valerie can't understand such a language. It strikes her as a fraud, as though God could be thus isolated and could speak from on high. She has already seen too many ideologies marked by such an all-powerful word delivered from on high.

But, then, what is the problem-complex? Some utter God's name, others make no mention of him. Some invoke him in certain practices and discourses even there where others efface him. Some seek something different from what they name, others seek for that which nevertheless they erase. Some say that it is God who gives sense to the language of man, others say that man can not receive a sense come from elsewhere. The writer on linguistics, J. Claude Milner, states:

> "The God of the philosophers and of the savants is this X that sets a limit to the Universe and from this fact constitutes it as a Whole, accessible to universalizing propositions. Whether this X be a reality or not matters little if existence is constructible from it: thus deism and atheism are equivalents."[11]

The man of today, when he is marked by the new mentality, is hardly tempted to give himself a deism or an atheism as reference points.

He will give wide berth to a knowledge or a construction of this kind. Of the one whose only recourse is to transcendalism, Valerie would say: "It just doesn't make sense!" For she has a presentiment that man cannot base himself on himself by constructing a place from which he derives his power and his validity, or by contesting this place called God out of a concern to establish himself by himself. Those who participate in the new mentality out of a dislike for creating illusions, above all about oneself, are enemies of this self-foundation. They are afraid that in speaking of God or in denying him one is speaking only of oneself. To them the language seems trap-laden, ambiguous or thin. In their opinion one can only speak of God with extreme modesty. God is wholly a poem and not a demonstration.

There is in this position of those who participate in the new mentality or rather in this exposition—in the sense of one "exposing oneself" to a risk—a certain opening in which the Christian faith can be lived more than in a culture that wants to be an ideal place of principles or a lowland of positivisms. There is a poetic truth that is different from the mere pragmatic-sufficient truth: it is a matter of letting be, of letting appear, of letting what was hidden come into view. Valerie was deeply affected by a poem that I lent her, a Polish poem forbidden over there:

> *"Our Father who is mute*
> *who does not respond to any appeal*
> *who makes us know only through the blasts*
> *of the whistles,*
> *every morning, that the world still exists,*
> *speak:*

This girl that takes the tram to her job,
in a shabby coat, three rings
on her fingers,
a trace of sleep still in her swollen eyes,
must hear your Voice, in order to awaken
in this dawn, one more time.

Our Father who knows nothing,
who does not even behold this earth,
who only through the morning newspaper
makes us know
that the world, our world persists
in good order,
behold:

This man seated at his table, bent
over a minced cutlet,
a liter of vodka and the newspaper greasy
with the sauce and the text,
must know that you know, you too,
he must know that you know, in order to
survive this day, one more time.

Our Father, who does not exist,
whose name nobody invokes any more,
save some didactic brochures
in which it is written without a capital
because the world muddles through without
you, be:

This man who goes to bed in order to sleep
and to make a list
of his lies, of his fears, of his
betrayals of today,
he must believe that you are, that you are
everything notwithstanding.
He must believe that you are in order to sleep
this night, one more time.'' [12]

Valerie, deeply affected, repeatedly read over this poem.
For her it is not a tiny gem that one possesses, that one can
keep closed tightly in one's hand, but a place with unlimited
perspectives and a place that is very humble. Christian faith,
always rooted somewhere, like a poem, with words that stum-
ble and nevertheless never cease to walk, that's something
that can interest her. Likewise with Jesus: the apostles had
seen someone who had their language and who nevertheless,
at the same time, was the Son of God. Later, the philosopher
Saint Justin, who had not seen Jesus in his time, was to say
that to be Christian is "to believe in God through Jesus
Christ," that is, through someone situated in a particular
epoch of history, in a particular place, in a particular
language, through someone who is in a "sector," a "se-
quence," a "segment."

What happens when some men say that they are the people
of God, recognized, privileged, exclusive, when they assert
that they have the sole God, the true God for themselves
alone? When some, within this group, say that in order to
have God with one's self, one must be in the desert alone with
God while others say that one must be up in arms for God,
and others still say that one must fulfill God's prescriptions
to the letter? What happens when other peoples, alongside
them, fashion all sorts of gods and establish themselves, each
one, as the whole of God? On a day like the others, a hidden
thing happens in an obscure place: it's called Bethlehem.

This new mentality that begins in our epoch, and which,
being weak, can be destroyed like an embryo, concerns itself
with non-sensational news items, with the individual
something. To proclaim the Christian faith in this culture is
to be able to say, because it's true, that the God of Jesus concerns himself with this "almost nothingness" which is a birth
somewhere, with this individual something which is each
human being and his or her everyday life. And this individual
something resists and will always resist the global system and

unwarranted universalizations. Valerie tells me: "Jesus, yes, but not the Church." She expressly states that she wants to fight with all her might an institution that has placed itself as though outside the individual, as the holder of the Truth in a totalitarian fashion, an institution that wants to teach from on high and exert pressure to impose itself, an institution that wants one to have the simple faith of the charcoal-burner and which claims to be the only one that provides the only talismans for avoiding solitude here below, exclusion, death itself. "The Church is not the good God," concludes Valerie who finds this institution infatuated with itself. "It's a false promise." To be sure, I find and I tell Valerie that her passionate and caricature-like position is "somewhat outdated." But for her it's important and she insists: she finds that men often make "false promises:" "A woman above all would always like to believe in promises, that is her great temptation. The ecclesiastical world has deceived women on their condition." The lucidity of Valerie's companions, male and female, rejects any naive docility. It will have no truck with any institution that is looking for militants. It would like the Church to be faithful to Bethlehem, that she be "eucharistic," multiplied in a humble and hidden way through a hundred places and a hundred cultures, strewn like flowers. And not contracted, constricted like a summit, like a power, like a pinnacle.

Valerie and her friends await from Christians a message in the language of Bethlehem, not a speech that would be a series of ready-made answers. Valerie and her friends can no loner endure those who come to them, saying: "We have answers." Bethlehem leaves a space to man and his questions, it is not a citadel or a seat prepared in advance. How would Christians be able to talk of God to Valerie and her friends and talk to her of a God to whom one listens, if these Christians themselves do not listen to the questions of men? Our contemporaries cannot listen to the God of Jesus if

Christians do not listen to the questions of men. And he who does not listen to men does not listen to God.

We can hardly reproach Valerie and her friends on this score. They deplore the fact that Christians are insufficiently faithful to what the ensemble of the Revelation shows them: that from Abel to Christ, true, innocent beings struggle for the liberation of their brothers and that Jesus comes, last, to close the list and to break the infernal circle in which men believe themselves to be imprisoned: the thought that they have a debt towards a superior crushing power and the acceptance of the existence of masters. Did not Jesus say, "Neither be ye called masters." A new enunciation of God, gratuitous and unusual, always springs up from the experience of liberation. It is always among those who try to liberate themselves and to liberate others, and not among the dead, that we much look for the Risen One.

The God of Jesus, and Valerie has a presentiment of this, is the one who accomplishes great deliverances. To be sure, by passing through the desert and exodus, the strange land and exile, but the liberation is at the end. She would want that Christians listen more, like God, to the calls for help from the men and the peoples of today, whether they are locked up in gulags or schizophrenias, and that they act.

Yes, Valerie is logical: she would like, through Christians, to meet the omni-impotence of a God who hides himself, who manifests himself modestly in the quotidian and the particular, a God who always articulates himself to a history, to a culture and a language, and to meet, at the same time, the strength of this God, a strength that springs up from this very weakness, like the Risen Christ who sprang up from the shadow of death. Then, perhaps, she herself will also recognize God.

But to recognize God is, first of all, to recognize that he has a weakness for man. And by virtue of this fact, when one is man, to have a true heart of man, to be a "relational" being as God knows how to be. Valerie's new mentality wants first and foremost to be relational, with no annexation of others, in acquiescence to an incessant pluralism. The question that Valerie poses to Christians is clear: are you going to accord a true freedom to your faith, the freedom to love, the taste for the relational, the vivaciousness of tenderness, the sharpness of look and the rejection of illusions? Will you dare to have a heart that has a weakness for man, that has a weakness for risks, for struggles against injustice, that has a weakness for others in their quest to live, to survive, to live better, in their hope of days beyond the night, and the dead. Are you going to construct places in which neither the word nor ready-made ideas are imposed, places where one, in communion, speaks with others of that which constitutes the cry of life, the cry of daily births, places where we trust each other, where we await the other ardently?

FOOTNOTES
Chapter I

1. Ed. Galilee, Paris: 1977.
2. François Chatelet, *La Quinzaine littéraire*, no. 143, 1972.
3. *Le Monde*, June 2, 1978.
4. *Le Monde*, June 1, 1978.
5. Ibid.
6. *Le don du rien*, Stock, 1977, pp. 144-145.
7. *Le don du rien*, Stock, 1977, p. 10.
8. Ibid. p. 182.
9. *La tolérance*, Gallimard, 1975, pp. 38-39.
10. *Des choses cachées depuis la fondation du monde*, Grasset, 1978.
11. *Le don du rien*, p. 204.
12. *Le don du rien*, p. 205.
13. Ibid. p. 287.

Chapter II

1. *Spiritual Autobiography of Charles de Foucauld*, edited and annotated by Jean-François Six. Trsl. by J. Holland Smith. P. J. Kenedy and Sons, New York, p. 212.
2. *Autobiography of a Saint: Thérèse of Lisieux*, trsl. by Ronald Knox, The Harvill Press, London 1958, p. 256.
3. Ibid. p. 256.
4. Ibid. pp. 253-54.
5. Ibid. p. 254.
6. Ibid. p. 256.
7. Ibid. p. 225.
8. Ibid. p. 257.
9. Ibid. p. 239.
10. Ibid. p. 239.
11. Ibid. p. 239.
12. *Approaches to the Gospel*, Paris, Seuil, p. 87.
13. A. Jaubert, *op. cit.* p. 98.

Chapter III

1. Gallimard, pp. 38-39.
2. *Nouvel Observateur*, March 22, 1977.
3. *Le Matin*, April 12, 1977.
4. *Le Matin*, April 18, 1977.
5. H. Bourgeois, *Dieu selon les chrétiens*, Centurion, 1974.
6. Ibid. p. 134.
7. Cerf, 1977.

8. (*Panorama of the Credo*), Desclée & Co.
9. *Op. cit.* p. 144.
10. C. Duquoc, p. 87.

Chapter IV

1. Cf. *Revue de la Philosophie positive* May-June 1880, pp. 321-322.
2. *Ce que je crois* (What I believe), Grasset, 1975, p. 31.
3. Ibid.
4. *L'avenir de l'intelligence (The Future of Intelligence),* p. 112.
5. (*Each in His Darkness*), Pantheon Books, 1961, p. 10.
6. *Introduction to Christianity* by Joseph Ratzinger. Burns & Oates, London, 1969, p. 17.
7. Ibid., p. 19.
8. *On Being a Christian* by Hans Küng, trsl. by Edward Quinn, Doubleday & Co., New York, 1976, p. 75.
9. Ibid., p. 76.
10. *L'imagination créatrice (The creative imagination),* Neuchâtel, La Baconnière, 1971, p. 282.
11. *Scénarios du futur,* Denoël, 1975.
12. *Utopie et civilizations,* "Champs libres," Flammarion.
13. *Nouvel Observateur,* December 1977.
14. July 29, 1978.
15. *Nouvel Observateur,* Decmeber 25, 1977.
16. *Le Monde,* September 8, 1976.
17. Ibid.
18. J. B. Pontalis, *Le Monde,* November 3, 1977.
19. J. B. Pontalis, *Le Monde,* November 3, 1977.
20. Christian Zimmer, *Temps modernes,* July 1978, p. 2314.

Chapter V

1. E. Fried, *Cent poèmes sans frontières* [One Hundred Poems Without Frontiers], Ch. Bourgeois, 1978.
2. *Concilium,* p. 117-118.
3. *Ibid.,* p. 117.
4. *Ibid.*
5. *ibid.,* p. 128.
6. *Recherches de Science religieuse,* 1975, pp. 457-504.
7. Cf. *La passion de comprendre,* Ed. du Centurion, 1977.
8. P. Valadier, *Les Études,* April 1976.
9. *Ibid.*
10. August 13, 1978.
11. J. C. Milner, *L'amour de la langue,* Seuil, 1978, p. 75.
12. Stanislaw Baranczak, *Respiration artificielle* translated by Constantin Jelenski and Jean-Paul Guibert, *La Quinzaine littéraire,* 16, on July 31, 1977, no. 260.